GIANTS
of Land, Sea & Air ·
Past & Present

DAVID PETERS

Alfred A. Knopf   New York

Sierra Club Books • San Francisco

GIANTS

of Land, Sea & Air ·

Past & Present

To all the scientists, authors, and illustrators that came before, I now see farther because I have stood on the shoulders of giants.

The author's special thanks to:
Dr. Kevin Padian, Department of Paleontology, University of California at Berkeley, for reading the manuscript and helping so generously; Danny Moses and Diana Landau at Sierra Club Books and Dinah Stevenson and Jenny Fanelli at Alfred A. Knopf.

THE SIERRA CLUB, founded in 1892 by John Muir, has devoted itself to the study and protection of the earth's scenic and ecological resources—mountains, wetlands, woodlands, wild shores and rivers, deserts and plains. The publishing program of the Sierra Club offers books to the public as a nonprofit educational service in the hope that they may enlarge the public's understanding of the Club's basic concerns. The point of view expressed in each book, however, does not necessarily represent that of the Club. The Sierra Club has some fifty chapters coast to coast, in Canada, Hawaii, and Alaska. For information about how you may participate in its programs to preserve wilderness and the quality of life, please address inquiries to Sierra Club, 730 Polk Street, San Francisco, CA 94109.

THIS IS A BORZOI BOOK PUBLISHED BY ALFRED A. KNOPF, INC.

Book design by Mina Greenstein

Library of Congress Cataloging-in-Publication Data   Peters, David. Giants of land, sea & air, past & present. Includes index. Summary: Discusses body size in the animal kingdom and depicts giants from past and present, both individual specimens and those belonging to large species such as the prehistoric giants. Includes gatefold pages showing the very largest animals. 1. Animals—Miscellanea—Juvenile literature. 2. Extinct animals—Miscellanea—Juvenile literature. 3. Body size—Miscellanea—Juvenile literature. [1. Body size. 2. Prehistoric animals. 3. Animals. 4. Toy and movable books] I. Title. II. Title: Giants of land, sea & air, past & present. QL49.P39 1986 591.4 86-2719
ISBN 0-394-87805-1   ISBN 0-394-97805-6 (lib. bdg.)

0   9   8   7   6   5   4

Cover illustration: sperm whale

Manufactured in Singapore

CONTENTS

INTRODUCTION

This is a book about giants—about many of the biggest animals ever to inhabit the earth's land, seas, and air. The giants are grouped according to either type or shape so that their similarities, differences, and peculiarities can easily be seen.

All of the illustrations have been drawn to the same scale (1 inch = 22½ inches). If you hold the book 18 inches from your eyes, the illustrations will seem the same size as the actual animal would seem when viewed from a distance of 33¾ feet. Even with the facts and figures in front of us, it can be difficult to realize how immense these creatures are or were, and so every two-page spread includes an illustration of an average-size adult human couple drawn to the same scale.

Of the living animals, only the largest single individuals on record have been pictured and described in this book. Encountering such giants—especially the marine animals—would be a rare or once-in-a-lifetime experience. However, for the prehistoric animals, the size estimates probably represent an average for the species. The odds against finding an abnormally gigantic specimen in fossil form are rather high because so few bones become fossils and so few fossils ever see the light of day.

The appearance of the prehistoric animals has been re-created by scientists and artists on the basis of several kinds of evidence: fossil skeletons; footprints; feather, scale, and skin impressions; cave paintings; and the actual frozen bodies of some Ice Age types. Educated guesswork by scientists as they piece together the remains, following the body plan of living animals, produces models and drawings of what the animal *may* have looked like. Not all scientists agree on how the evidence should be interpreted. The drawings in this book are based on a number of different sources and views.

Each animal has two names, a common name that everyone uses and a Latin name with which scientists describe it. Many prehistoric creatures have no common name and so only the Latin one is used. Under each headline in this book, the Latin name (in italics) is in two parts, indicating the genus and the species of the giant described in the text. The remaining words (separated by dots) identify the animal's order, class, and phylum, the main branches of the family tree of the animal kingdom.

There are two kinds of giants.

Some are individual creatures that during their lifetime grew abnormally large for their species.

This condition is known as gigantism and, in mammals, it often arises from an overactive pituitary gland. This gland releases the hormones necessary for growth and other bodily processes. Fish, amphibians, reptiles, and some mammals, such as the elephant, may grow continuously throughout their lives, and so giants of these species are usually old individuals. Disease, inadequate food supply, inadequate defense against predators and parasites, the loss of the last set of renewable teeth, and accidents may shorten the life of these animals, limiting the species' potential size.

Other creatures are, by nature, just plain huge. These giants are the species that have evolved slowly, the end product of countless generations, each a little larger than the generation preceding it.

The process of evolution sometimes favors the development of ever larger individuals. Mating privileges are often won by the biggest and strongest male or the one with the largest horns, antlers, or tusks. And this male is likely to pass his genes on to a greater number of offspring than his rivals. These offspring in turn may produce generations of ever larger individuals, each one a little better able to defend itself and exploit its environment than its competitors.

Large, healthy animals have a greater chance to reproduce because they stand less chance of being attacked. Predators are more likely to attack the smaller, weaker members of a herd, weeding out the sick and infirm because they make an easier kill.

Environment, too, plays a role in the development of giants. When living conditions remain favorable for long periods of time, animals tend to thrive. But when a stable environment is upset by drastic weather changes, cosmic catastrophes, loss of living space, the evolution of inedible food, or the introduction of more successful predators, the highly specialized giants are likely to be the first to disappear. No one knows why the dinosaurs died out 65 million years ago, but one theory suggests that all of the above, to a greater or lesser degree, occurred simultaneously over a 10-million-year period and killed off all the giant animals on the earth. Today, Africa's living giants—the gorilla, elephant, and rhinoceros—are finding their chances for survival diminishing rapidly as civilization takes over more and more of their homes.

Bigger animals stay warm more easily than

smaller ones. In order to stay quick and alert, animals must keep their internal systems within a fairly narrow temperature range. A small animal's internal organs are just inches from the variable outside air temperature. But a large animal's vital organs may be buried many feet deep within the insulating bulk of its own body. Like elephants and whales, the bigger dinosaurs maintained a fairly constant and efficient body temperature simply by being so large. They stored the day's heat deep within their huge bodies, radiating little of it away throughout the chilly night. Whales are insulated from the bone-chilling polar seas by the sheer bulk of their immense blubber-clad bodies.

Sea creatures are free of one major thing that limits the size of land creatures—gravity. The weight of an animal increases as it grows three-dimensionally: taller, wider, and deeper. But the support of the legs can only increase in two dimensions, width and depth, and bone is not strong enough to take the strain after a certain point. Sea creatures are about as dense as seawater and so are buoyed up by the sea itself. Some have even added weight to insulate and streamline their bodies.

In the air, excess weight is a hindrance. The largest flying birds and reptiles were hollow-boned soarers with gigantic wingspans that could catch rising air currents and fly to great heights with a minimum flapping of their wings.

Many times in the history of life, giants have had the advantage. But after humans entered the scene, being big became a detriment to many species. Humans were cunning enemies that hunted in packs, used weapons and traps, and valued the largest animals in order to store up food reserves, trade the surpluses, and increase their status within the tribe. Giant animals today must compete with the ever-growing human population for the last of the wild lands remaining to them.

Most of the animals in this book lived and died before modern humans evolved. Some animals became extinct during our early years on this planet. Others may disappear in the near future unless we decide they are too valuable and too wonderful to lose.

This book is not all-inclusive. Some incredibly huge creatures (such as the alleged 200-foot giant octopus) have not been included because their existence has not yet been proved beyond a reasonable doubt. Others are known to have existed, but the available evidence (single bones) is so limited that we can't begin to guess at their appearance.

New giants will continue to be discovered in the future as fossils continue to be unearthed and the remains of seagoing giants occasionally wash ashore from the ocean's depths. Some of the biggest animal giants to ever grace this earth have been discovered only recently. These discoveries are forcing scientists to reevaluate their assumptions about the natural limits of life on the earth. In other words, there's a lot more to be learned about giants.

GIANTS

of Land, Sea & Air ·
Past & Present

Human

Homo sapiens • Primates • Mammalia • Chordata

The tallest living primates, modern humans evolved in Africa at least two million years ago. With wide variation, adult males average 5 feet 9 inches in height. The average weight is 162 pounds. Females are usually shorter and lighter. The tallest man reliably measured grew to a height of 8 feet 11 inches and weighed more than 400 pounds. The heaviest man reliably measured weighed 1,069 pounds but was less than 6 feet tall.

Unlike other primates, which include monkeys and gorillas, humans stand erect and have virtually naked skin. A number of skin colors and hair textures occur among the races. Humans eat both plants and animals.

Humans have lived for as long as 120 years, but 70 is the modern average. They mature sexually at about age 12. Gestation is 9 months. Babies are born helpless and generally weigh 6 to 10 pounds at birth.

Humans are not particularly fast or ferocious, but they are the most intelligent of all animals and have become skillful tool and weapon makers. They organize themselves into societies, constructing elaborate shelters and cities as well as complicated devices that enable them to travel faster, fly higher, and swim deeper than any other animal. They were the first animals to walk on the moon.

Gigantopithecus

Gigantopithecus blacki   [extinct]
Primates • Mammalia • Chordata

Gigantopithecus (jie-gan-toe-PITH-uh-kuss) was a ground-dwelling plant eater of the Himalayas during the Pliocene (two million years ago) in India and the Pleistocene (500,000 years ago) in China. Known only from fossil teeth and jawbones, this primate was not an ancestor of humans but was similar to them in some ways. The largest *Gigantopithecus* jawbones are larger than those of any known gorilla yet are shaped like those of a human, with small canine teeth and a rounded chin. From the size of the jaws, scientists have deduced that, standing upright, *Gigantopithecus* was 8 feet tall, with a probable weight of 600 pounds. Males were considerably larger than females. Some people who believe in the existence of the elusive "abominable snowman" suggest that it may be a form of *Gigantopithecus* still living today.

Gorilla

Gorilla gorilla • Primates • Mammalia • Chordata

The gorilla, on the average, is the largest of living primates, measuring up to 6 feet 2 inches tall and weighing up to 683 pounds. Males typically weigh 450 pounds. Females are always smaller. Gorillas live in tropical rain forests in western Africa in societies of from 2 to 30 individuals. They are nomadic and eat 30 to 40 pounds of fruit, vegetables, and meat that they forage each day. Female gorillas reach sexual maturity at age 7 and males at age 10. A gorilla may live as long as 35 years. Gorillas were first discovered by modern scientists in 1847. They have no natural enemies other than humans, who hunt them for food and cut down their forests.

HUMAN   GIGANTOPITHECUS   GORILLA

Andrewsarchus

Andrewsarchus mongoliensis   [extinct]
Carnivora • Mammalia • Chordata

Andrewsarchus (an-drooz-AR-kuss) was named for Roy Chapman Andrews, the famous fossil hunter. Probably measuring over 6 feet tall at the shoulder and 16 feet long, this primitive, wolflike predator may have been the largest meat-eating land mammal ever. Because only a 3-foot-long skull of this giant has been found, guesses about the rest of its body are based on the appearance of smaller, better known, related species with similar skulls.

Although related to the doglike carnivores of the period, huge *Andrewsarchus* may have moved about more slowly, like a modern bear. To support such a big skull, *Andrewsarchus* must have had a strong neck. Like others of its kind, it may have had a deep, heavily muscled chest supported by forelimbs ending in rounded nails, unlike the sharp claws of almost all other meat-eaters. Lacking claws, *Andrewsarchus* may have been a carrion eater. Some scientists think it fed on tough vegetable matter.

Its powerful jaws were filled with huge teeth capable of tearing flesh and crushing anything from bone to mollusk shells. The snout was long and narrow, like a wolf's, but it broadened immensely at the cheekbones. Judging by the skull, the muscles that worked the jaws must have been enormous. *Andrewsarchus* lived 40 million years ago during the late Eocene epoch. Its fossil skull was discovered in Mongolia and described in 1924.

Kodiak Bear

Ursus arctos • Carnivora • Mammalia • Chordata

This subspecies of the wide-ranging brown bear is found only on Kodiak Island, off the Alaskan coast. It is the largest meat-eating land mammal alive today. A male may be up to 10 feet long from nose to tail and weigh up to 1,656 pounds. The average Kodiak bear is 8 feet long, stands 4 feet 4 inches high at the shoulder, and weighs 1,175 pounds. Females are always smaller. At birth the young are rat-sized and helpless.

Unlike other carnivores, bears will eat plants as well as meat, and the Kodiak bear may eat 20 pounds of fish, small animals, plants, and honey each day. Despite its tremendous size and its huge claws and teeth, the Kodiak does not tackle large prey. It is not typically aggressive, but it can be extremely dangerous when provoked. A Kodiak may rise on its hind legs and shuffle toward an opponent in an awesome display, but unless it is cornered or is protecting its young, it will probably flee. Kodiak bears usually live less than 30 years in the wild. They have no natural enemies but humans.

ANDREWSARCHUS

KODIAK BEAR

African Elephant

Loxodonta africana
Proboscidea • Mammalia • Chordata

The largest living land animal is the African elephant. Males, called bulls, may measure up to 13 feet 2 inches tall at the shoulder and weigh nearly 27,000 pounds, but they average 11½ feet tall and 14,000 pounds. A prehistoric *Loxodonta* measured more than 14½ feet tall at the shoulder, making it the largest of all elephants.

The African elephant's ears are up to 4 feet wide, the largest ears in the world. This animal also has the largest teeth: tusks that grow up to 8 feet long and may weigh 80 pounds each. Its trunk, which is 6 feet long and weighs 300 pounds, is an especially sensitive "nose" that can also pick up small or large objects and hold 1½ gallons of water. The elephant's huge skull is thick but not solid; an extensive network of air holes makes it lightweight. On the soles of the elephant's feet is a thick spongy material that cushions each step.

Elephant calves are born after a 20- to 22-month gestation, the longest in nature. They are 3 feet tall and weigh 200 pounds at birth. Although elephants continue growing throughout their lives, after age 60 their molars are no longer renewed. Lacking the ability to chew their food, they starve to death. An adult consumes up to 600 pounds of grass, leaves, branches, and bark and up to 50 gallons of water each day. Elephants are good swimmers.

African elephants travel in family herds of 5 to 50 or more and are highly protective of their calves. Males travel separately. Healthy adults have no enemies other than humans, but the young, aged, and sick are prey for various carnivores.

AFRICAN ELEPHANT

Woolly Mammoth

Mammuthus primigenius   [extinct]
Proboscidea • Mammalia • Chordata

The woolly mammoth reached a maximum height of 14 feet at the shoulder, but averaged only 11 feet tall. This Ice Age elephant was covered with a thick layer of fat and a heavy coat of shaggy fur. The enormous curved tusks that grew up to 16 feet long and crossed in front were used as snow plows to uncover mosses and grasses. Twigs of conifers, willows, birches, and alders have been found in the stomachs of frozen mammoth carcasses. The woolly mammoth built up food supplies in the form of a hump of fat on its shoulders to help it survive the long, cold winters.

Mammoths first appeared in India during the Pliocene epoch, three million years ago. During the Pleistocene Ice Age, one million years ago, woolly mammoth herds crossed the land bridge from Siberia to North America. Mammoths were hunted and held in awe by the primitive humans living among them. Some European cave paintings depict the woolly mammoth as the artist saw it in life. The last mammoth died out only 10,000 years ago. Frozen flesh and bones were first discovered by scientists in 1799.

WOOLLY MAMMOTH

Arsinoitherium

Arsinoitherium zitteli   [extinct]
Embrithopoda • Mammalia • Chordata

Arsinoitherium (ar-suh-noy-THEE-ree-um) lived from 35 to 28 million years ago during the Oligocene epoch in Northern Africa and China. It was named for Arsinoe, an Egyptian city near the area where its fossils were discovered in 1900. *Arsinoitherium* was 11 feet long and 5½ feet high at the shoulder. It had four horns on its head, two massive ones in front and two smaller ones farther back, above the eyes. The male's front horns were long and sharp; the female's were shorter and rounder. Although ferocious looking, *Arsinoitherium* was a sluggish, plant-eating swamp dweller. It is rather distantly related to the elephant family despite its superficial resemblance to the rhinoceros. *Arsinoitherium* is the only member of the entire order of Embrithopoda yet discovered, and so far has no predecessors or ancestors in the fossil record.

Brontotherium

Brontotherium platyceras   [extinct]
Perissodactyla • Mammalia • Chordata

Brontotherium (bron-toe-THEE-ree-um) was the largest of the brontotheres (also known as titanotheres), a line of mammals that developed from the same tiny ancestors as our modern horse from 50 to 25 million years ago during the Eocene and Oligocene epochs. *Brontotherium* grew to 15 feet in length and was 8 feet high at the shoulder. It had a very small brain encased in a huge skull and a broad, two-pronged horn above its nose, longer and broader on the male. The horns seem to have been used in ramming contests, as some of the fossils of the adult males have broken ribs that appear to have been bashed in just such a way. The animal's legs were short and its skeleton massive. Although the leg bones were nearly solid to support the weight of the animal, the skull was like a hard sponge, filled with tiny air holes that lightened it. An elephant's skull is much the same.

As a grazing animal, *Brontotherium* would have had trouble cropping grasses with its weak front teeth and so may have had a prehensile lip and/or a long tongue to help tear the grass out of the ground. *Brontotherium* fossils have been found in great numbers throughout midwestern North America and in Asia and Europe, where the animal ran in herds.

ARSINOITHERIUM

White Rhinoceros

Ceratotherium simus
Perissodactyla • Mammalia • Chordata

The white rhinoceros, also known as the square-lipped rhino, is the largest of the five species of rhinoceros alive today. Growing up to 15 feet long and 6½ feet high at the shoulder, the white rhino may weigh 7,000 pounds. The average white rhino is usually only 5½ feet at the shoulder. The two horns on its snout are as hard as bone but in fact consist of compressed, hairlike fibers that grow throughout the rhino's lifetime. The foremost horn can reach a length of 62 inches. Females have longer horns than males. With its wide mouth, the white rhino prefers to graze on grasses; the name "white" is a mispronunciation of the word "wide." The related black rhino is actually the same light gray color as the white rhino but has a pointed prehensile lip used to strip leaves off bushes.

The white rhinoceros inhabits dry country. Its thick, hairless skin offers no protection from biting insects, so the rhinoceros frequently wallows in mud or takes dust baths for relief. The white rhinoceros is often solitary but may form small herds. Gestation is up to 17 months after which a single hornless calf is born. The calf stays with its mother for over 2 years and is sexually mature at age 5. A rhinoceros's life span is 70 years.

The white rhino is bad-tempered in the wild. Confronted with objects that appear threatening, it will charge, reaching speeds of 30 miles per hour. There are only about 2,000 white rhinoceroses left in central Africa. The animal has been hunted nearly to extinction due to excessive demand for its horn, which in some societies is deemed to have medicinal and decorative value.

BRONTOTHERIUM   WHITE RHINOCEROS

Indricotherium

Indricotherium transouralicum [extinct]
Perissodactyla • Mammalia • Chordata

Indricotherium (in-druh-koe-THEE-ree-um) was the largest land mammal of all time, weighing as much as 66,000 pounds. This peaceful plant-eater, a hornless rhinoceros, was 18 feet high at the shoulder and 37 feet long. It could reach leaves and twigs 25 feet off the ground with its long neck. Like the black rhinoceros today, *Indricotherium* may have had an upper lip that came to a finger-like prehensile point for grasping leaves, twigs, and branches. It was built rather narrowly, with long legs and stubby toes resting on huge, spongy, resilient pads to help spread the enormous weight. *Indricotherium* (also known as *Baluchitherium* and *Paraceratherium*) lived 20 million years ago during the Miocene epoch in Baluchistan, an area in south-central Asia. Its fossils were first discovered in 1908.

INDRICOTHERIUM

Dinohyus

Dinohyus hollandi [extinct]
Artiodactyla • Mammalia • Chordata

Dinohyus (die-noe-HIE-uss) means "terrible hog." Larger than any other known pig, this aptly named animal was 7 feet tall at the shoulder and 11 feet long and must have weighed 2,000 pounds. It lived during the Miocene epoch about 25 million years ago and is believed to have been closely related to the modern hog.

Like modern hogs, *Dinohyus* had a flat, sensitive snout and probably a keen sense of smell. Its knobby skull was 3 feet long, sporting huge, tusk-like canine teeth. Males had larger tusks, indicating that *Dinohyus* used them as weapons, as do modern hogs. The tusks were also used for digging: *Dinohyus* was a root eater. It had four toes on each foot, the middle two forming hooves and the outer two not touching the ground—the same as modern-day pigs. *Dinohyus* fossils are fairly common and are found throughout the northern hemisphere.

DINOHYUS

Giraffe

Giraffa camelopardalis
Artiodactyla • Mammalia • Chordata

The giraffe is the tallest of all living land animals, averaging 17 to 18 feet tall. The largest may stand nearly 20 feet tall and weigh 4,000 pounds. Giraffes, related to the deer family, have lived in Africa since the Miocene epoch 15 million years ago.

On the top of its head a giraffe has two short, bony knobs, covered with skin and hair, and a bump in the middle of its skull. With eyes on either side of its upraised head, the wary giraffe has a clear view of its surroundings. Although its neck is 6 feet long, a giraffe has only 7 neck vertebrae, the same number a human has.

The main food of the plant-eating giraffe is acacia leaves, which it plucks from thorny branches with its 18-inch prehensile tongue. After a 14½-month gestation, a colt 6 feet tall and weighing 110 pounds is born. It reaches sexual maturity in 3 to 4 years. In herds of 15 to 70, giraffes travel on the open savannas, moving at a top speed of 32 miles per hour. They spar by swinging their long necks against one another and fight by kicking, but their first defense is to run from their enemies, the lion and the hyena. Giraffes have a 20-year life span in the wild.

GIRAFFE

Alticamelus

Alticamelus altus [extinct]
Artiodactyla • Mammalia • Chordata

Alticamelus (al-tuh-KAM-uh-luss) means "high camel." Modern camels may reach 7 feet tall. At 18 feet tall, *Alticamelus* is the tallest camel yet discovered. *Alticamelus* lived 20 million years ago, during the Miocene epoch, in Asia and North America. It was a tree-browsing animal. Its stilt-like legs and long thin neck helped *Alticamelus* get at leaves no other animals could reach.

Alticamelus was the first species to show the camel's unique spreading feet. Most hooved mammals stand on the last joint of their toes. Camels stand on the last and next to last joints. Thick pads beneath the toes cushion each step and enable the animal to walk on loose sand. A camel's hump is made entirely of fat and acts as a reservoir to sustain the animal when food and water can't be found. *Alticamelus* may have had a hump of fat like a camel's, but we may never know. So far, only fossils of the animal's bones have been discovered.

Moose

Alces americana
Artiodactyla • Mammalia • Chordata

The moose, the largest deer ever, is found in North America. A bull moose can grow up to 7 feet 8 inches tall at the shoulder and may weigh up to 1,800 pounds. Cows are generally smaller and do not have antlers.

Each year the bull sheds his antlers and grows a new pair. The antlers, which can spread more than 6 feet across, are used when the bulls spar for mating privileges. The mating bellow of the bull moose can be heard for 3 miles or more. One or two calves, 32 inches tall at birth, are born after a 7½-month gestation period. The moose grazes on soft twigs, water lilies, mosses, and lichens in marshes near forests. It is a fine swimmer. The moose is generally a peaceful browser but is unpredictable and can be dangerous. Its enemies are bears, cougars, and humans.

ALTICAMELUS   MOOSE

Giant Ground Sloth

Megatherium americanum   [extinct]
Edentata • Mammalia • Chordata

The giant ground sloth was a peaceful, tree-browsing mammal that lived during the Pliocene and Pleistocene epochs from 10 million up to only 10,000 years ago. Its 24-foot length made it almost invulnerable to attack by the smallish predators of its time. Newly arriving humans may have hunted the giant ground sloth to extinction.

Native to South America, this massive animal was able to push trees over by brute strength to get at leaves too high to reach. It probably used its long, curved claws to hook low branches and bring them close to its long tongue. Its claws were so long that it had to walk on its knuckles.

Doedicurus

Doedicurus clavicaudatus   [extinct]
Edentata • Mammalia • Chordata

Doedicurus (dee-duh-KYEW-russ) was the largest of the glyptodonts, a family of armadillolike mammals that lived in the Western Hemisphere during the Pliocene and Pleistocene epochs 10 million to 1 million years ago. *Doedicurus* was 14 feet long, with a 5½-foot-high shell.

Unlike the armadillo with its shell of horny skin, glyptodonts had a shell made of bone, unique among mammals. The thick invulnerable armor covered the head, back, and tail. Stiff, coarse hairs stuck out at joints in *Doedicurus*'s armor wherever skin was exposed. The animal had short, massive legs and strong claws for digging. It was a peaceful plant eater with small, peglike teeth. The long tail, ending in a macelike spike, was an effective defensive weapon that could be swung at attackers.

GIANT GROUND SLOTH

DOEDICURUS

Great Gray Kangaroo

Macropus giganteus
Marsupialia • Mammalia • Chordata

The great gray kangaroo is the largest of all living marsupials—mammals with pouches for their young. The largest males may measure 8 feet 8 inches from head to tail and stand 7 feet tall. They may weigh up to 200 pounds. Females are usually about half as large.

With its huge, muscular hind legs, this kangaroo can broad-jump 25 feet or, at full speed, leap 40 feet with each bound, using its long, thick tail as a counterbalance. Each hind foot has four toes—one much larger than the others, with a dangerous claw, and a smaller toe right beside it. The other two toes, growing side by side, are so tiny they don't reach the ground and are used like a comb for grooming. Great grays travel in mobs, browsing on leaves and twigs, rather than grazing the grasslands like the related red kangaroo.

After a 33-day gestation, the young are born as tiny, hairless embryos. Only an inch long, blind, and without hind legs, they manage to crawl without assistance to the mother's pouch, where a milk-filled nipple awaits them. There they stay for up to 8 months while they continue to develop. The great gray kangaroo has a life span of up to 15 years in the wild. Found only in Australia, kangaroos first came to the attention of modern science in 1770.

Giant Kangaroo

Macropus ferragus   [extinct]
Marsupialia • Mammalia • Chordata

The giant kangaroo was 10 feet tall. It lived in Australia from 1 million years ago until only 10,000 years ago. Humans arrived in Australia 12,000 years ago and hunted this animal to extinction.

Castoroides

Castoroides ohioensis   [extinct]
Rodentia • Mammalia • Chordata

Castoroides (cass-toe-ROY-deez), the giant beaver, grew to 10 feet long, including its 3-foot tail. Beavers evolved in North America 35 million years ago, with *Castoroides* appearing about 2 million years ago. It survived until 10,000 years ago, making it a contemporary of early humans.

Other than size, *Castoroides* shared many physical traits with its 3-foot-long present-day counterpart. Proportionately *Castoroides* had smaller feet and legs than modern beavers but a similar flattened, scale-covered tail. While modern beavers prefer to chisel tree bark with their sharp teeth, the blunt teeth of *Castoroides* seem to have been designed for uprooting cattails and other water plants.

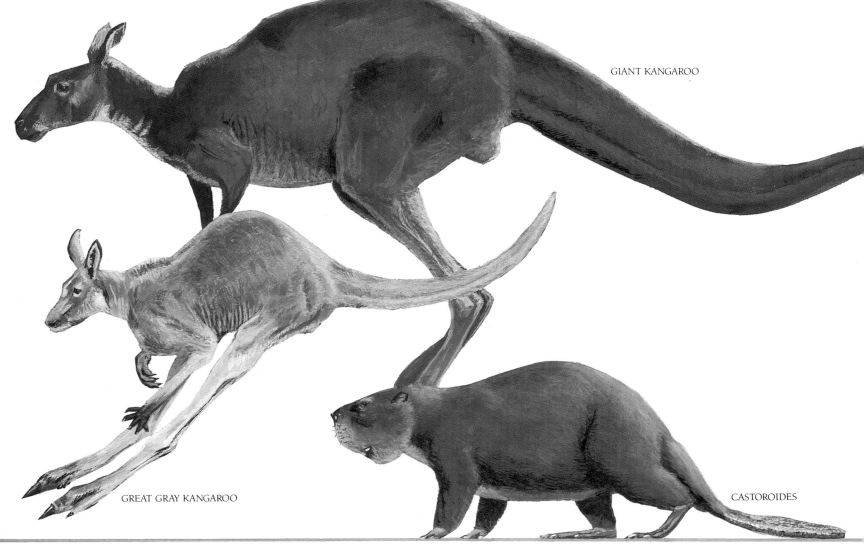

GIANT KANGAROO

GREAT GRAY KANGAROO

CASTOROIDES

Moa

Dinornis maximus [extinct]
Struthioniformes • Aves • Chordata

The flightless moa was the tallest bird ever, reaching a height of 13 feet. Although some weighed as much as 520 pounds, moas this big were rare. Moas evolved from smaller, flying birds on the islands of New Zealand during the Pliocene epoch, 10 million years ago. There were no predators to impede their increase until humans arrived on the islands 1,500 years ago.

Moas became extinct only 300 years ago. They are known from the thousands of skeletons left by natives of New Zealand who ate these birds until none were left. Moas, ostriches, and other similar running birds form a group called the ratites, characterized by their flat, keel-less breastbone. Moas had long necks, tiny heads, and strong legs but lacked wings entirely. They did not have flat interlocking feathers, like other birds. Instead, those that covered the wings and body were soft and shaggy. Moas ate fern roots and green shoots and built nests of leaves and grasses.

Phorusrhacos

Phorusrhacos longissimus [extinct]
Phorusrhacid • Aves • Chordata

Phorusrhacos (for-uss-RAK-uss), formerly known as *Phororhacos*, was a predatory flightless bird that stood as tall as 10 feet but averaged between 5 and 8 feet in height. It had a head larger than a horse's. Its wings were tiny and useless for flying. In the absence of any large reptilian or mammalian predators, this bird went unchallenged as the largest meat-eater in South America from the Oligocene into the Pliocene epoch, 38 million to 4 million years ago. Undoubtedly, it was a swift creature. With its long, strong legs; long, sharp claws; and huge, powerful, hooked beak— supremely adapted for tearing flesh— it ran down and devoured small reptiles, mammals, and birds.

MOA

PHORUSRHACOS

Gallimimus

Gallimimus bullatus   [extinct]
Saurischia • Reptilia • Chordata

Gallimimus (gal-ee-MIE-muss), at 30 feet long, was a giant ornithomimid, a group of dinosaurs named for their similarity to ostriches. All had small, toothless skulls; large eyes; slender bodies; thin, flexible necks; and long, spindly sprinter's legs. Experts believe they were among the fastest dinosaurs, able to reach speeds of up to 40 miles per hour. They escaped predators by running.

Living in Asia during the late Cretaceous period, from 70 to 65 million years ago, *Gallimimus* inhabited dense cypress forests. There it may have combed through grass and low plants with its clawed forelimbs, looking for eggs and small animals and snapping up anything that tried to scurry away. Its fossils were discovered in 1972.

GALLIMIMUS

North African Ostrich

Struthio camelus
Struthioniformes • Aves • Chordata

The tallest bird alive is the ostrich. Although it may grow up to 9 feet tall and weigh as much as 345 pounds, the ostrich typically averages 7 to 8 feet tall and weighs 200 to 300 pounds. It lives on the dry, dusty plains of Africa and western Asia.

The ostrich has long legs, a long neck, and a smallish head. Males are black with white wing tips and tail plumes. Females are dull gray or brownish. The necks and heads of both sexes are lightly feathered with down, but the legs are completely naked.

Unlike all other birds, which have three walking toes on each foot, the ostrich has only two, one larger than the other. It can run at speeds upward of 40 miles per hour using its short wings (which are useless for flying) to help lift some of its weight off the ground. The ostrich can also defend itself against predators by inflicting disabling kicks with its powerful legs.

The ostrich travels in bands of up to 50 individuals, often with herds of zebra and antelope. It is a plant eater but will consume small birds and insects as well.

Ostrich eggs are up to 8 inches long and weigh nearly 4 pounds each, the largest of any living bird. The male scoops out hollows in the ground, where the female lays up to 10 eggs. Then they share incubating duties. When hatched, chicks are already the size of barnyard chickens, and they reach full size in 6 months. Ostriches may live up to 62 years.

NORTH AFRICAN OSTRICH

Allosaurus

Allosaurus fragilis   [extinct]
Saurischia • Reptilia • Chordata

Allosaurus (al-uh-SOR-uss) was a two-legged meat-eating reptile averaging 30 feet in length. Some specimens from North America grew as large as 42 feet, as big as any of the largest-known dinosaur predators, including *Tyrannosaurus rex.*

Allosaurus was the largest meat eater of the Jurassic period, living 150 to 136 million years ago. It was probably an active hunter and may have hunted in packs. *Allosaurus* could tear out the entrails of its victims with its huge fangs and the sharp claws on its forelimbs and feet. Fossils of this dinosaur have been found worldwide.

Reticulated Python

Python reticulatus
Squamata • Reptilia • Chordata

The largest snake, perhaps of all time, is the reticulated python, a legless reptile that reaches a maximum length of 32 feet 9 inches and a weight of 450 pounds. Its name derives from the reticulation or netlike pattern of camouflage markings covering its body.

A good swimmer, the reticulated python lives in southeast Asia. The female coils around her eggs and, unlike most reptiles, generates body heat to help incubate them. When hatched, the young are already 3 feet long. A fully grown reticulated python can swallow animals as large as sheep. To do this, it first kills its prey by wrapping its coils tightly around the victim to keep it from breathing. Then it opens its extendable jaws and slowly engulfs the prey whole, starting at the head. The meal may take several months to digest. Heat-sensitive grooves under the nose help the python detect warm-blooded prey, even in total darkness. Reticulated pythons may live for 20 to 30 years.

ALLOSAURUS

TANYSTROPHEUS

RETICULATED PYTHON

Jonkeria

Jonkeria truculenta   [extinct]
Therapsida • Reptilia • Chordata

At 14 feet long, *Jonkeria* (jon-KERR-ee-uh) was the largest and one of the earliest of the therapsids, the order of reptiles that ultimately evolved into mammals. *Jonkeria* itself was not a direct ancestor of mammals but was an important food source for those that were. Living in South Africa during the late Permian period, 230 million years ago, *Jonkeria* had sharp canine fangs and small grinding cheek teeth. As a plant eater, it needed a huge stomach to digest its food. Taking advantage of its size, blimplike *Jonkeria* was able to keep warm and active in cooler climates and was among the first plant-eating vertebrates to live outside the equatorial regions. On top of its skull, *Jonkeria* retained a third eye called a pineal eye, also found in primitive fish and amphibians. This eye probably helped therapsids regulate body temperature by sensing daylight and weather changes.

Tanystropheus

Tanystropheus longobardicus   [extinct]
Protorosauria • Reptilia • Chordata

Tanystropheus (tan-ee-STROFE-ee-uss) was an extraordinarily proportioned reptile with a stiff 18-foot neck that was more than half the total length of this 35-foot animal. The vertebrae were stiffened along the entire length of the neck by slender rods that interlocked one bone with another. The long neck may have helped a small *Tanystropheus* to catch insects and small animals climbing through trees. Young 2-foot-long specimens had three-pronged teeth, ideal for catching insects. Older individuals developed sharp conical teeth for snaring fish. With its sprawling legs keeping it propped in place, *Tanystropheus* may have lain on a rocky outcropping of seacoast, occasionally dipping its long neck into the water for a meal.

Tanystropheus, which was discovered in 1852, lived in Europe during the early Triassic period, 225 million years ago — 20 million years before the first dinosaurs appeared. Its legs turned out to the sides, unlike dinosaur limbs which are set perpendicular to the ground.

JONKERIA

Tyrannosaurus

Tyrannosaurus rex   [extinct]
Saurischia • Reptilia • Chordata

Tyrannosaurus (tie-ran-uh-SOR-uss) was the largest meat-eating land animal of all time, measuring up to 45 feet from nose to tail. This dinosaur could have stood 18 feet high and weighed as much as 15,000 pounds.

Tyrannosaurus used its long tail as a counterbalance to its huge torso and head. It had a cavernous mouth filled with knife-sharp, serrated teeth up to 7 inches long. It may have attacked large prey by running at it with jaws wide open. The skull was reinforced to withstand tremendous impacts. With its huge, three-clawed hind feet planted firmly on the ground, *Tyrannosaurus* tore its victims apart with its teeth. Its ribs formed a cage covering its chest and belly as a protection against the lunges of thrashing victims. Its front legs were very tiny for such a giant animal; they could not even reach the mouth and were probably useless.

Tyrannosaurus lived in North America at the very end of the Cretaceous period, 65 million years ago. Its fossils were discovered in 1902 and have been found only in Montana.

TYRANNOSAURUS

Spinosaurus

Spinosaurus aegypticus   [extinct]
Saurischia • Reptilia • Chordata

Spinosaurus (spine-uh-SOR-uss) was a 40-foot-long, 14,000-pound meat-eating dinosaur found in mid-Cretaceous Africa, about 110 million years ago.

Possibly living in hot, open country, *Spinosaurus* evolved a set of long, bony spines that stood 6 feet high from the backbone. The spines may have supported a sail of skin that acted as a temperature regulator, according to some scientists. Lined with hundreds of blood vessels stretched over the hugely extended spines, this sail might have helped *Spinosaurus* to warm up or cool off just by changing its orientation to the sun. When the sail faced the sun, it would have warmed up. The blood vessels in it would have distributed the warmed blood throughout the body. During the hottest part of the day, when *Spinosaurus* wanted to cool off, it might have turned the sail edge-on to the sun, minimizing the heating effect and allowing cool breezes to draw heat away from the radiating sail.

With its long, strong arms, *Spinosaurus* may have walked on all fours to help conserve energy. It may have been an active hunter but was probably a scavenger. Its teeth were straight, not curved backward to hold struggling prey like those of other meat-eating dinosaurs. Fossils were discovered in Egypt in 1915.

SPINOSAURUS

Ankylosaurus

Ankylosaurus magniventris   [extinct]
Ornithischia • Reptilia • Chordata

Ankylosaurus (an-kie-luh-SOR-uss), a 35-foot-long giant, was the largest of the ankylosaurs, the four-legged armored dinosaurs. It may have also been the widest dinosaur of any type. In the past, ankylosaurs have been pictured as sprawling and slow-moving. Recent evidence suggests they were probably swift and agile, like a rhinoceros. *Ankylosaurus* ranged across western North America during the Cretaceous period 70 to 65 million years ago.

Like *Doedicurus* (page 14), *Ankylosaurus* was a peaceful plant eater with tiny teeth, but it was built like a tank from head to tail. Its triangular head ended in thick spikes. Thick, oval plates of bone and numerous thick spikes attached to leath-ery skin protected the animal's back and sides. The skin was embedded with bony studs. Plates of bone were plastered over the skull. Even the eyelids were armored with bone. The tip of its stiff tail ended in a club of bone that could be swung at attackers or mating rivals. It could have knocked a tyrannosaur to the ground, possibly breaking its attacker's leg or hip in the process, which would have been fatal. *Ankylosaurus* was probably invulnerable unless turned over on its back by attack or accident. Its fossils are rare but are always found upside down. The first *Ankylosaurus* fossil was discovered in 1908.

ANKYLOSAURUS

Stegosaurus

Stegosaurus stenops   [extinct]
Ornithischia • Reptilia • Chordata

Stegosaurus (stegg-uh-SOR-uss) was the largest of the stegosaurs, the four-legged, plant-eating, plated dinosaurs. Living in the Jurassic period 140 million years ago, *Stegosaurus* grew to 32 feet long and may have weighed as much as 6,000 pounds.

Stegosaurus had two rows of flat plates running down its back from head to tail. The plates were imbedded in the skin and were not directly attached to bone, so scientists can't tell from the fossils whether the plates grew side by side or were staggered. Like the presumed sail of *Spinosaurus* (page 21), the plates seem to have been temperature regulators. Supplied with hundreds of tiny blood vessels, their large surface areas could warm the blood when face-on to the sun or cool the blood as air currents passed over them. They may have served as a defense against meat-eating dinosaurs as well.

The tail of *Stegosaurus* ended in two pairs of formidable spikes that could have been swung at hungry predators. The long, small, narrow skull contained a walnut-size brain, which has led some scientists to label *Stegosaurus* perhaps the stupidest dinosaur, but in fact its brain was quite adequate for its needs. *Stegosaurus*'s head was held low so it could browse on ferns and other types of low ground cover. It chopped off vegetation with its toothless horn-covered beak but, lacking chewing or shearing teeth, swallowed its food quickly. In its huge stomach the food could ferment for days while being crushed by stones *Stegosaurus* had deliberately swallowed. Stegosaurs seemed to have disappeared at the beginning of the Cretaceous period, interestingly at the same time that ankylosaurs were becoming more plentiful. *Stegosaurus* fossils, first discovered in 1877, have been found in North America.

STEGOSAURUS

Lambeosaurus

Lambeosaurus lambei   [extinct]
Ornithischia • Reptilia • Chordata

Lambeosaurus (lam-bee-uh-SOR-uss) was named in honor of its discoverer, Lawrence Lambe. A 56-foot skeleton recently unearthed on the Baja California peninsula establishes *Lambeosaurus* as the largest of the hadrosaurs, or duck-billed dinosaurs.

Lambeosaurus lived during the late Cretaceous period, around 80 million years ago. Like other hadrosaurs, it had a broad, toothless beak like a duck's, but farther back along the jaws it had flattened packs of grinding teeth to chew the tough foods in its diet. As the teeth wore out they were replaced by others growing in vertical columns from the jaws. An adult's skull might contain 2,000 teeth at a time! From fossilized stomach contents we know *Lambeosaurus* ate pine needles, oak and poplar leaves, and succulent water weeds.

Lambeosaurus's skull was topped by a hatchet-shaped crest of hollow bone, an extension of the nasal passages leading to the windpipe. The crest may have acted as a resonating chamber to amplify roars and mating calls. It may also have greatly increased this reptile's sense of smell by providing a greater area to hold receptors. The crest was smaller and rounded on females and young.

Lambeosaurus usually walked on its four limbs and could have walked on two, balanced by its long, stiff, broad tail. It may have swum by sweeping its tail from side to side. Fossils were first discovered in 1923.

LAMBEOSAURUS

Triceratops

Triceratops horridus   [extinct]
Ornithischia • Reptilia • Chordata

Triceratops (trie-SER-uh-tops) was the largest of the ceratopsians, plant-eating reptiles with a bony collar frill and a beak like a parrot's. The largest *Triceratops* was a 12,000-pound dinosaur, 30 feet long and 9½ feet tall at the shoulder. Its skull was 7 feet long with 3½-foot-long horns. The collar frill helped to defend the animal from attack and also anchored the large jaw muscles that enabled its curved beak and shearing teeth to crush the tough new plants then evolving. Like cattle, two *Triceratops* may have locked horns to push and shove each other until one conceded defeat. *Triceratops*'s forelimbs were probably held straight under the body in usual dinosaur fashion rather than stuck out to the sides, as they have usually been pictured. With straight legs *Triceratops* could have run as fast as 30 miles per hour.

Triceratops was one of the commonest dinosaurs in North America toward the end of the Cretaceous period and one of the last of the giant dinosaurs to become extinct, about 64 million years ago. Fossils were first discovered in 1877.

TRICERATOPS

Apatosaurus

Apatosaurus ajax   [extinct]
Saurischia • Reptilia • Chordata

Apatosaurus (app-uh-toe-SOR-uss), also known as *Brontosaurus,* was one of the largest diplodocids, dinosaurs with long necks, long tails, and forelimbs shorter than their hind limbs.

Apatosaurus grew to 75 feet long, with a 20-foot neck and a 30-foot tail. Its enormous weight of up to 60,000 pounds was supported by an arched

LAMBEOSAURUS (cont.)

backbone of hollow vertebrae held aloft by massive, nearly solid leg bones. Like an elephant, *Apatosaurus* had a single nasal opening, located high on its head between its eyes.

With its peglike teeth, it snipped off swamp vegetation and pine needles, swallowing everything whole because it had no chewing teeth. Like birds and crocodiles, *Apatosaurus* deliberately swallowed rough-edged stones to help grind food inside its stomach.

Apatosaurus seems to have been a land dweller that occasionally went into the water. It lived in North America during the late Jurassic period, 140 million years ago, and was among the commonest land animals of its day. From fossil footprints we know it moved in herds with the adults surrounding the young to protect them. Fossils were first discovered in 1877.

Brachiosaurus

Brachiosaurus branchi   [extinct]
Saurischia • Reptilia • Chordata

Brachiosaurus (bray-kee-uh-SOR-uss) was the largest, longest, and heaviest land animal of all time. A recent specimen found in Colorado, unofficially dubbed *"Ultrasaurus,"* is known from only a few bones; they suggest the animal was more than 100 feet long, stood 60 feet high, and weighed as much as 100,000 pounds. *Brachiosaurus* existed from 150 to 130 million years ago during the last of the Jurassic period and earliest Cretaceous.

It is the largest of the brachiosaurs, a family of long-necked plant-eaters with high shoulders, and forelimbs longer than their hindlimbs, giving their backs a characteristic down slope.

A full-grown *Brachiosaurus* was protected from predators by its great bulk. It retained heat by the sheer mass of its body and may have cooled off by wading into water. With its long neck, it could reach high leaves that no other dinosaur could touch. *Brachiosaurus*'s nostrils were placed on a crest on top of its head, perhaps so that it could breathe while drinking. The crest may have increased *Brachiosaurus*'s sense of smell or acted as a resonating chamber for mating calls.

Its hind feet were broad, with a pad on the bottom that flattened and spread to cushion each step. Fossils of *Brachiosaurus* were first discovered in 1903 in East Africa and have since been found in Europe as well as North America.

BRACHIOSAURUS (cont.)

APATOSAURUS (cont.)

Mamenchisaurus

Mamenchisaurus hochuanensis [extinct]
Saurischia • Reptilia • Chordata

Mamenchisaurus (mah-MEN-chee-SOR-uss) was named for the town of Mamenchi, in China, where its fossils were discovered. This 72-foot-long dinosaur is distinguished by its extremely long neck.

The neck, made of 19 vertebrae (more than in any other dinosaur), was held fairly rigidly by a series of overlapping bones for more than half its 35-foot length. It was more flexible only near the small head and where the neck attached to the chest. The best guess is that *Mamenchisaurus* held its head aloft and reached into trees for food. Some scientists think it could have stood on its hind legs to reach the highest vegetation. *Mamenchisaurus* lived in the late Jurassic period in Asia, some 150 million years ago. Fossils were first discovered in 1954.

MAMENCHISAURUS

BRACHIOSAURUS

APATOSAURUS

Giant Condor

Argentavus magnificens [extinct]
Falconiformes • Aves • Chordata

The giant condor, a South American vulture, had the largest wingspan of any bird ever, estimated at 23 to 25 feet, twice that of modern condors. The giant condor lived during the Pleistocene epoch a million years ago. Fossilized bone fragments were discovered in 1979, from which scientists have reconstructed a bird nearly identical to the California condor except in size.

The giant condor was probably a carrion eater. Carrion, the carcasses of dead animals, is filled with the bacteria of decay and is poisonous to most living animals, but the giant condor would have been well adapted to deal with it. Its digestive system could probably kill bacteria. Vultures eat by poking their heads into bloody, open carcasses. The giant condor's head was likely bare of feathers so that it would dry quickly and be exposed to the purifying effects of sunlight. The giant condor must have lived near areas with permanent soaring conditions and stayed aloft for hours on its enormous wings, relying on its sharp eyesight to guide it to dead and dying animals.

Prionosuchus

Prionosuchus plummeri [extinct]
Temnospondyli • Amphibia • Chordata

Prionosuchus (pree-oe-noe-SOOK-uss) was the largest amphibian that ever lived and the largest land animal of the Permian period, 230 million years ago. Discovered in 1972 in northern Brazil, the fossilized bone fragments of this 30-foot-long amphibian indicate it resembled a present-day gavial, a type of crocodilian. Its extremely long and narrow tooth-lined jaws made an efficient fish trap.

Some scientists think *Prionosuchus* was entirely aquatic. After hatching from eggs laid in the water, its young lived like fish, using gills to breathe.

QUETZALCOATLUS

Quetzalcoatlus

Quetzalcoatlus northropi   [extinct]
Pterosauria • Reptilia • Chordata

Quetzalcoatlus (ket-sahl-koe-AHT-luss), named for Quetzlcoatl, the Aztec plumed-serpent god, was the largest flying animal of all time. It had a wing-span, estimated from bone fragments, of between 35 and 40 feet. This pterosaur must have weighed about 150 pounds. It had a long neck, a sharp beak, and no skull crest. The arm and leg bones of *Quetzalcoatlus* were twice as long as *Pteranodon*'s and some of its neck bones were seven times as long.

Quetzalcoatlus lived 65 million years ago on the plains of Cretaceous Texas. Like a modern soaring bird, it probably waited until late morning for the hot sun to stir up rising currents of warm air, called thermals. It could catch one of these with only a few flaps of its gigantic wings. The thermal would lift it high in the air, giving it an excellent view of its territory. Some scientists think that *Quetzalcoatlus* was a carrion eater. Others suggest that it waded along the shallows of ponds and lakes, spearing fish and other animals with its long, toothless jaws. Fossil remains were first described in 1975.

Deinosuchus

Deinosuchus hatcheri   [extinct]
Crocodilia • Reptilia • Chordata

Deinosuchus (die-nuh-SOOK-uss), also known as *Phobosuchus,* was the largest crocodilian of all time. It may have been as long as 52 feet and may have weighed 27,200 pounds. The largest modern crocodiles, presently the largest living meat eaters on land, may reach up to 20 feet long but average 15 feet long and 900 to 1,200 pounds.

Deinosuchus lived during the late Cretaceous period, 80 million years ago. It had a 6-foot-long skull and heavy, platelike scales. Except for its teeth, which were larger but fewer in number than a modern crocodile's, it likely had the same proportions, habits, and diet as today's animal. Living near coastal land in tropical and subtropical waters, it probably laid its eggs in nests on land. *Deinosuchus* would have swum like other crocodiles, using its tail in a side-to-side serpentine motion. It could probably run over land for short distances but likely spent most of its time sunning itself, digesting a meal, or lazing about at the surface of the warm water.

With nostrils on the tip of its snout and eyes on the top of its head, *Deinosuchus* could breathe and see while almost completely submerged. It could sneak up and attack unwary wading dinosaurs. Like most reptiles, it had no chewing teeth and would have swallowed huge chunks of food whole. *Deinosuchus* could reduce large prey to bite-sized pieces by clamping it securely in the jaws and viciously twisting and whipping it about in the water until the victim fell apart, as crocodiles do today.

GIANT DRAGONFLY

Giant Dragonfly

Meganeura monyi   [extinct]
Odonata • Insecta • Arthropoda

Meganeura (megg-uh-NYEW-ruh) was a giant prehistoric dragonfly with the largest wingspan of any insect ever known: 28 inches from tip to tip. Fossils of *Meganeura* were found in Carboniferous-period rocks dating from 280 million years ago.

Apart from its gigantic size, *Meganeura* looked exactly like a modern dragonfly, with a long, slender body and two pairs of transparent, veined wings. If *Meganeura* resembled modern dragonflies in other respects, it may have flown at speeds of up to 60 miles per hour. *Meganeura* held its legs underneath its body as a basket so that it could trap airborne insects and eat them in flight.

A young *Meganeura* hatched from an egg and began life as a meat-eating, wingless, underwater nymph. Its extendable jaws could reach out half the length of its body to snatch prey. Growth occurred through repeated shedding of the skin. After a few years, the nymph crawled onto a rock or water plant above the surface of the water for its last shedding. The skin along its back split open, revealing a winged adult *Meganeura,* ready to fly, eat, and mate.

MAMENCHISAURUS (cont.)

DEINOSUCHUS

Pteranodon

Pteranodon ingens   [extinct]
Pterosauria • Reptilia • Chordata

Pteranodon (ter-AN-uh-don) was a tremendous pterosaur—a flying reptile—with a wingspan of up to 24 feet. It had a 6-foot-long head, including a 27-inch crest. *Pteranodon* probably weighed only 36 pounds.

    Pteranodon's wings were thin membranes of skin connected along its body to its hip and out to its greatly elongated fourth "finger." The wing membranes were reinforced by long, flat fibers that gave the wing strength. *Pteranodon*'s hollow bones made the animal so lightweight that it could simply stretch out its wings and soar in light sea breezes. Its bony crest, which was only ⅛ inch thick in places, jutted from the back of its skull, acting as an aerodynamic balance to its long, toothless beak. Flying over Cretaceous oceans 90 million years ago, *Pteranodon* plucked shelled squids, fish, and other small animals from the sea and stored them in a small pouch under its throat.

    Scientists think *Pteranodon* was probably warm-blooded, able to make its own body heat instead of just absorbing heat from its surroundings as most reptiles and other cold-blooded animals do. This guess about *Pteranodon* is based on the fact that furlike impressions have been found in the fossils of similar pterosaurs. Fur and feathers are insulating materials presently found only on warm-blooded animals.

    Pteranodon may also have been light-colored or white. As it stretched its wings while flying under the hot sun, a light coloring would have helped it stay cool by not absorbing the heat as dark colors do. Also, a white underside helps flying animals blend in with the sky and not scare the surface fish that were *Pteranodon*'s main source of food. Fossils were first discovered in the 1860s and continue to be discovered in Kansas and Nebraska.

PTERANODON

Elasmosaurus

Elasmosaurus platyurus   [extinct]
Sauropterygia • Reptilia • Chordata

Elasmosaurus (ee-laz-moe-SOR-uss) was the largest of the plesiosaurs, seagoing reptiles with long necks, smallish heads, and limbs that had evolved into flippers. *Elasmosaurus* reached a length of 47 feet. Its snaky 25-foot neck was more than half the length of its body and had up to 71 vertebrae. *Elasmosaurus* held its long, flexible neck ready to catch any fish unfortunate enough to swim by. Its mouth was an effective fish trap, filled with teeth so long and sharp they stuck out to the sides when it closed its jaws.

Elasmosaurus lived 80 million years ago in Cretaceous seas. It was a fast, agile swimmer. Scientists believe *Elasmosaurus* could paddle backward, forward, or in circles equally well. It is not known whether *Elasmosaurus* returned to land to lay eggs or gave birth to live young at sea. First described in 1868, fossils have been found in North America.

ELASMOSAURUS

KRONOSAURUS

Kronosaurus

Kronosaurus queenslandicus [extinct]
Sauropterygia • Reptilia • Chordata

Kronosaurus (kroe-nuh-SOR-uss) was the largest of the pliosaurs, seagoing reptiles with short necks, large heads, and feet that had evolved into flippers. *Kronosaurus* was 56 feet long, including its 12-foot-long jaws lined with 80 sharp, conical, 9-inch-long teeth. It swam in Australian seas during the Cretaceous period, 100 million years ago.

Kronosaurus was a powerful long-distance swimmer. It may have dived nearly 1,000 feet to catch ammonites, once common, free-swimming, squidlike creatures with spiral shells. *Kronosaurus*'s flippers moved like the wings of a penguin, up and down against the water. Huge muscles twisted and pulled the flippers back like wings, helping *Kronosaurus* "fly" through the water, gaining speed on both the upstroke and the downstroke. *Kronosaurus*'s lower breastbones, ribs, and hip girdle formed a hard basket of bone that served both to protect its vulnerable underside from attack and to securely anchor its huge swimming muscles.

Kronosaurus breathed air and must have returned to the surface frequently to do so. Because of the animal's huge size it is improbable that females returned to land to lay eggs, in the manner of sea turtles. Perhaps they gave birth in shallow ocean waters where their young could rise quickly to the surface for a first breath.

KRONOSAURUS (cont.)

Shonisaurus

Shonisaurus popularis   [extinct]
Ichthyosauria • Reptilia • Chordata

Shonisaurus (shone-ee-SOR-uss) was the largest of the ichthyosaurs, marine reptiles that typically had fishlike tails and tall dorsal fins. *Shonisaurus* measured at least 50 feet in length, including a 10-foot-long skull, and may have weighed up to 80,000 pounds.

Ichthyosaurs evolved from the earliest reptiles, perhaps from a type that had never actually ventured onto land. Ranging in size from 2 feet long to 50 feet long, ichthyosaurs evolved fishlike shapes in order to be better adapted to their marine environment. Like whales, they breathed air through nostrils situated only slightly below and in front of their large eyes. Their long beaks were filled with sharp teeth for catching the fast-swimming fish they ate. Ichthyosaur females retained their eggs inside the body until they hatched.

Living during the Triassic period, 220 million to 180 million years ago, *Shonisaurus* was the largest animal on earth. It had a relatively long head, teeth embedded in sockets, and tail bones only slightly bent downward to support a triangular tail fin. The eyes of *Shonisaurus* were 12 inches in diameter and ringed with overlapping bones to prevent the eyeball's collapse under the pressure of deep water.

Giant ichthyosaurs became extinct by the mid-

SHONISAURUS

dle of the Jurassic period, 190 million to 130 million years ago, replaced by more advanced, smaller, swifter types with tail vertebrae more sharply bent to support a crescent-shaped fishlike tail. These, too, gradually died out, 80 million years ago. Ichthyosaur fossils have been found worldwide since the early 1800s. *Shonisaurus* fossils were discovered in Nevada in 1928.

Oarfish

Regalecus glesne
Lampridiformes • Osteichthyes • Chordata

The oarfish, a rarely seen eel-like fish measuring 25 feet or more in length and weighing up to 600 pounds, is considered the longest bony fish in the sea. Bony fish have skeletons made of true bone, not cartilage, as is the case with sharks and rays. Oarfish 50 feet long have been seen but not captured. The oarfish's silvery, ribbonlike body may be more than 1 foot broad but edge-on is so thin and fragile as to seem nearly translucent in places.

Oarfish live in deep waters, feeding on the small fish that are found there. The crown on its head with long, arcing filaments can be raised or lowered at will. The long, thin, oarlike pelvic fins give the oarfish its name. Swimming with a wavy, side-to-side motion, the oarfish sometimes carries its head above the surface of the water. This practice may have given rise to the legend of the sea serpent.

Beluga

Huso huso
Acipenseriformes • Osteichthyes • Chordata

The beluga, or Russian sturgeon, is the largest freshwater fish in the world, measuring up to 24 feet long and weighing up to 3,250 pounds. The average is about half that size.

The beluga is a bottom feeder, pushing through the muck on the sea floor with its snout and sensitive, whiskery-looking feelers, called barbels, in search of marine worms and mollusks. Its large, tubular lips extend and suck the meal into its mouth.

Belugas show many characteristics of more primitive fish. The skin is armored with rows of bony plates. The skeleton is bone and cartilage, and the back vertebrae extend into the upper lobe of the tail fin, as do a shark's. Found only in the salty Black and Caspian seas, belugas migrate up the freshwater Volga River to mate and lay eggs, as many as 7.7 million at a time. Although their life span may be as long as 70 years, belugas are becoming rarer as their eggs continue to be eaten by humans as caviar.

SHONISAURUS (cont.)

OARFISH

Ocean Sunfish

Mola mola
Tetraodontiformes • Osteichthyes • Chordata

The ocean sunfish is the heaviest bony fish. It can weigh as much as 5,017 pounds and measure 14 feet from top to bottom, between the tips of its two fins. Sunfish average 8 feet between the fin tips and 2,000 pounds in weight.

Shaped like a flattened disk, the ocean sunfish uses its huge, fleshy, supple upper and lower fins to propel it slowly through the water. The tail has almost completely disappeared. The sunfish's skeleton is useless and practically nonexistent. Under its skin is a layer of tough gristle several inches thick which supports the fish's body and serves the same purpose as the skeleton in other animals. The tough, leathery skin of the sunfish is scaleless and covered with thick mucus and flat spines. Its mouth is small but filled with teeth. It feeds on crustaceans and jellyfish.

The ocean sunfish lays 300 million eggs at a time, more than any other animal. When hatched, the young are ⅛ inch long and shaped like spiny spheres. Not until they grow to over an inch long do they begin to resemble their parents.

OCEAN SUNFISH

MANTA RAY

SWORDFISH

Manta Ray

Manta birostris
Rajiformes • Chondrichthyes • Chordata

The manta, or devil, ray is the largest living ray. A ray is a flattened relative of the shark and, like the shark, has a skeleton made of cartilage and several gill openings. A manta ray can measure up to 22 feet from wing tip to wing tip (the average is 20 feet) and may weigh up to 3,500 pounds. The manta is a peaceful, nocturnal plankton eater and is not dangerous to humans.

The manta has the largest brain among fish. It swims by flapping its great wings through the water. Its top side is dark brown to black; underneath it is creamy white. The color comes off easily, so spots of white may occasionally be seen on the backs of mantas. Flaps near the manta's mouth, called cephalic fins, are used to help direct food toward its mouth. The manta's whiplike tail carries no stinger, unlike that of its relative the stingray.

The manta is found in both the Atlantic and the Pacific oceans. Although most rays prefer to stay hidden under a layer of sand at the bottom, the manta swims and feeds near the surface and has been seen leaping completely out of the water, sometimes in unison with others, and falling back to the sea with a thunderous clap. During such leaps, females sometimes give birth to their young in midair. (As in many sharks and other fish, the eggs are retained within the body of the female until hatching.)

COMMON SAWFISH

Swordfish

Xiphias gladius
Perciformes • Osteichthyes • Chordata

The swordfish may grow up to 15 feet long and weigh as much as 1,200 pounds, but it averages 7 feet long and 250 pounds. It can often be found sunning itself at the surface in the warmer latitudes of both the Atlantic and the Pacific oceans.

The swordfish is one of the world's fastest fish, traveling at speeds of up to 40 or 50 miles per hour. When a swordfish encounters a school of small fish or squid, it quickly flays its sword among them, returning soon after to devour the maimed prey. The sword, a flattened extension of the upper jaw, can reach a length of 5 feet. Immature swordfish have slender upper and lower jaws that are equally long and filled with teeth. But as the swordfish matures, the upper jaw continues to grow, shedding its teeth and becoming a sharp-edged sword. Adult swordfish have no teeth.

Common Sawfish

Pristis pectinata
Rajiformes • Chondrichthyes • Chordata

The common sawfish, also known as the small-tooth sawfish, is a ray that resembles a shark. Like other rays, it has its mouth and gill openings on the underside of its body. A sawfish may grow up to 25 feet long and weigh 1,200 pounds. It is found close to shore in shallow, tropical waters over sand or mud and may even ascend some rivers.

The sawfish has a long, flat snout that extends far beyond its underslung mouth and is studded with up to 32 pairs of teeth. As in sharks, the teeth grow out from the skin rather than the jaws. A young sawfish is born alive with its saw sheathed in a skinlike sack that is shed shortly after birth. The sawfish grubs for food in the sand and mud, using the saw as a probe. It may also slash schools of fish with its saw, then circle back to eat the mangled victims.

Great Shark

Carcharadon megalodon [extinct]
Squaliformes • Chondrichthyes • Chordata

This giant prehistoric cousin of the great white shark is known only from its teeth, discovered in 1873, which are identical in shape to those of a modern great white shark but are twice as large as the largest, up to 6 inches long. Judging by the teeth alone, the great shark's length has been estimated at up to 55 feet and its weight at up to 50,000 pounds. It lived in oceans of the Miocene epoch, some 20 million years ago, eating anything that swam, including huge prehistoric whales. It was the largest meat-eating fish of all time.

Sharks evolved 350 million years ago and have changed very little in all that time. All sharks are primitive fish with skeletons of pliable cartilage, not true bone, which evolved later.

Unlike those of most other vertebrates, a shark's teeth do not grow out from the jaws but from the skin. The teeth move forward as they increase in size, finally replacing the old, worn-out teeth at the edge of the shark's jawline. The skin itself is covered with thousands of tiny tooth-shaped scales, called denticles, that are as rough as coarse sandpaper. The denticles protect the shark and help it move more easily through the water.

GREAT WHITE SHARK

GREAT SHARK

Great White Shark

Carcharodon carcharias
Squaliformes • Chondrichthyes • Chordata

The great white shark is the largest living meat-eating fish. One specimen measured 29 feet 6 inches long, weighed 10,000 pounds, and had 3-inch teeth. Adults average 15 feet long and 1,700 pounds. The young are born alive, 4 feet long, and hungry.

The great white shark has been found in all the warmer oceans since the Cretaceous period, 100 million years ago. It can swim at speeds of up to 25 miles per hour. It is mainly a surface feeder, but occasionally it ventures deeper in search of prey. Because of a special organ in its circulatory system, the great white shark is one of only four fish considered to be warm-blooded. The great white has a keen sense of smell and is incredibly sensitive to vibrations in the water, especially the movements of an erratically fluttering wounded fish or a swimming human. It feeds on fish, other sharks, sea lions, sea turtles, and now and then on humans. The shark's digestive juices are strong enough to blister human skin. The great white's teeth are triangular, serrated, and so sharp they can cut a 750-pound fish in two with one bite.

WHALE SHARK

Whale Shark

Rhincodon typus
Squaliformes • Chondrichthyes • Chordata

The whale shark is the largest fish in the sea—as big as some whales, which is how it got its name. One specimen harpooned in 1919 measured 60 feet 9 inches and weighed 80,000 pounds. Whale sharks today rarely reach 41 feet and 42,000 pounds, and 20 to 30 feet is the average length.

The whale shark is the only shark with its mouth at the tip of its head instead of underslung beneath the nose. It has a distinctive checkered pattern on its back. Harpoons have bounced off its 4-inch-thick skin, thicker than that of any other animal.

The whale shark feeds on plankton while it breathes. Like all fish, it breathes by gulping water and expelling it through gill openings behind its mouth. As the oxygen-rich water passes over the gills, oxygen is exchanged for waste gases through the walls of the tiny blood vessels lining the gills. As the whale shark swims quietly through plankton-rich seawater with its 6-foot-wide mouth open, the tiny plankton are trapped by gill rakers, fingerlike projections that extend from its 10 gills back to the throat.

The whale shark lays the largest eggs of any animal, rectangular egg cases 12 inches long. When the young hatch, they are only 14 inches long. Whale sharks were first seen and recorded in 1828 and are found in all the warmer seas.

GREAT SHARK (cont.)

WHALE SHARK (cont.)

Basking Shark

Cetorhinus maximus
Squaliformes • Chondrichthyes • Chordata

The basking shark is the second-largest living fish, reaching a length of 40 feet and a weight of 32,000 pounds, although the average is 26 feet in length and 10,250 pounds. Like the whale shark, the basking shark is a quiet, nonaggressive plankton eater, filter feeding in the same way. It is found in cooler waters than the whale shark, often with its mouth and huge gills ballooning wide open as it gulps tremendous volumes of seawater. The enlarged gill openings on either side of the basking shark's body extend so far around they almost meet each other at the center of its back and under its throat.

BASKING SHARK

48

WHALE SHARK (cont.)

Greenland Shark

Somniosus microcephalus
Squaliformes • Chondrichthyes • Chordata

The Greenland shark grows up to 21 feet long and may weigh as much as 2,250 pounds, but averages only 10 feet in length. It is the only shark to live year-round in the polar waters of the North Atlantic. Also known as the sleeper, it seems to be an extraordinarily sluggish shark, living near the bottom of the sea, and rising only to feed. It is a mystery how this shark captures its food, which includes fast-moving fish, seals, and whales. The Greenland shark is almost always found with one white parasitic crustacean attached to each of its eyeballs. Up to 3 inches in length, these parasites may blind the shark but they may also lure small fish near the shark's jaws. Presumably the Greenland shark scavenges the carrion of dead whales and seals. The Greenland shark bears live young.

BASKING SHARK (cont.)

GREENLAND SHARK

Great Hammerhead Shark

Sphyrna mokarran
Squaliformes • Chondrichthyes • Chordata

The hammerhead is a large shark that may measure up to 18 feet 4 inches long and may weigh up to 1,860 pounds. The average size is closer to 12 feet and 1,000 pounds.

The hammerhead gets its name from its unusual head. It has eyes on the ends of the flattened extensions of its skull, but sensing electrical impulses and smelling blood are more important than vision to a shark. A shark will wave its head back and forth to sense which nostril smells a trail of blood more strongly, following its nose to its prey. The hammerhead's nostrils are also positioned near the tips of its head, making this shark perhaps the one most sensitive to the smell of blood.

The hammerhead swims near the surface of warm waters, feeding on small fish and squid, but its favorite food is the stingray. It finds them buried beneath the sand by sweeping its wide head back and forth like a metal detector sensing minute electrical impulses that betray the stingray's presence. The hammerhead has been known to attack its own kind as well as humans.

GREAT HAMMERHEAD SHARK

Sperm Whale

Physeter macrocephalus
Cetacea • Mammalia • Chordata

The largest meat-eating animal ever was a sperm whale bull 67 feet 11 inches long, weighing more than 144,000 pounds. In the past, bulls (males) may have grown to 84 feet long. Fossils of sperm whales are known from the Miocene epoch, 23 million years ago, making them among the most ancient of modern whales. The average modern bull measures 47 feet long and weighs 74,000 pounds. Females, known as cows, are always much smaller.

The sperm whale's 20-pound brain is the heaviest in the animal kingdom. The sperm whale takes the deepest dives of any known animal: from the surface of the sea it can dive 10,000 feet or more and stay below for nearly two hours before coming up for its next breath. Making up the bulk of the head is a huge reservoir filled with oil and a waxy substance called spermaceti, the source of the whale's name. Spermaceti may aid in buoyancy or in sonar. The sperm whale can "see" in total darkness with sonar, a process of sending out high-pitched sounds and listening for the echo as the sound bounces off objects. The skull reservoir seems to focus the sound impulses. Spermaceti also absorbs nitrogen from the bloodstream to help the whale avoid "the bends," a paralyzing disorder caused by the release of nitrogen bubbles into the blood after surfacing too quickly from a deep dive.

The sperm whale's long, narrow jaw has two

filter feeder. But a blue whale has an extendable "throat" with furrows that expand like an accordion to admit a tremendous quantity of seawater for filtering. The water flows through a hole below the whale's tongue to fill the throat bag. Then, plugging the hole with its tongue, the whale rises upside down to the surface to let gravity drain the accumulated seawater out of the bag and through the baleen filters in its mouth, where plankton is trapped. Emptied of seawater and streamlined, the whale may measure 12 feet deep from top to bottom; filled, it can swell to an incredible 36 feet deep, with a capacity of nearly 34,000 cubic feet (a six-fold increase in the whale's total volume). An adult may consume 16,000 pounds of plankton a day.

The blue whale is found in all the oceans. Its whistle is the loudest sound any animal makes: reaching 188 decibels, louder than a jet engine at takeoff, it can be heard 530 miles away. After being hunted nearly to extinction, the blue whale is now protected by law.

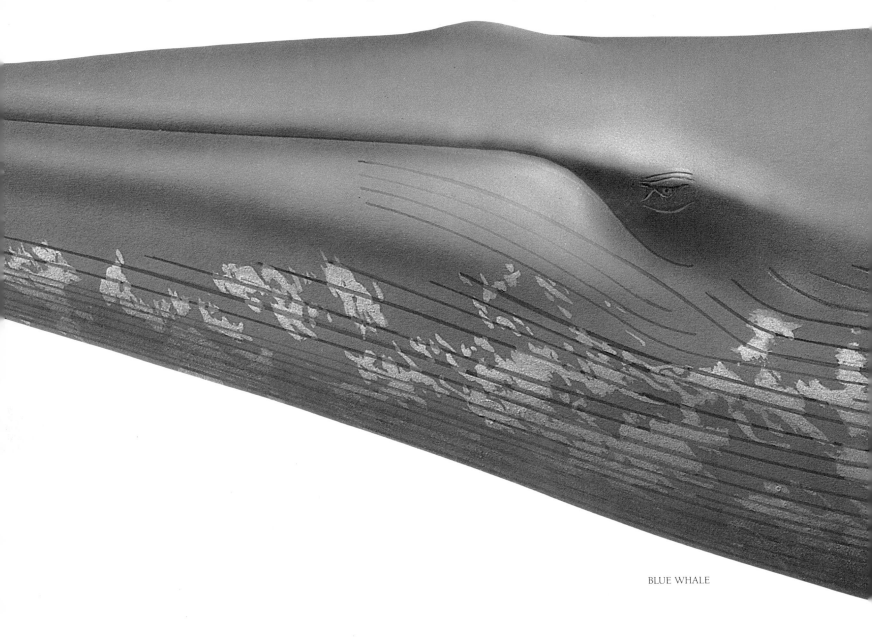

BLUE WHALE

KILLER WHALE

SPERM WHALE

rows of up to 56 nearly identical 8-inch conical teeth that fit into holes in the toothless upper jaw when the jaws close. The sperm whale eats many kinds of fish and sharks but its favorite food is the giant squid, which it finds at great depths and eats whole. Sperm whales often sport dozens of circular scars caused by the saw-toothed edges of the squid's suckers. Sperm whales live in groups called pods which may include several hundred animals. The bull sperm whale, unlike most other whales, collects a harem of females. Gestation is 18 months. A newborn sperm whale may measure 6 feet long. Sperm whales are found today in all oceans and are protected by law.

Killer Whale

Orcinus orca • Cetacea • Mammalia • Chordata

The killer whale is the only whale that kills other whales. It is the largest dolphin, the toothed whales with snouts more or less elongated to form beaks. A bull can measure 25 to 32 feet in length and weigh up to 20,000 pounds. The cow is smaller. The bull also has a larger and straighter dorsal fin than the cow.

Killer whales have up to 48 large, conical teeth and feed on salmon, seals, polar bears, and penguins, as well as whales. They attack in packs of from two to several dozen and often toss their victims around in play before eating them. They have never been known to attack a swimming or boating human.

Like other dolphins, the killer whale is an extremely intelligent animal, affectionate to its own kind. Family groups, called pods, include several generations. The killer whale communicates, finds food, and avoids obstacles by means of echolocation, or sonar. Killer whales are found in all the cooler oceans. Next to humans, killer whales are the longest-living mammals, with a life span of up to 100 years. They have no natural enemies other than humans.

Blue Whale

Balaenoptera musculus
Cetacea • Mammalia • Chordata

The blue, or sulfur-bottom, whale is the largest and heaviest animal of all time. Reaching a length of up to 110 feet 2 inches, a blue whale may weigh up to an estimated 508,000 pounds, or about as much as 3,135 average men. The average blue runs 80 to 90 feet and weighs 340,000 to 480,000 pounds.

The blue whale has been around since the Pliocene epoch, 9 million years ago. It is a tremendously strong mammal; the last third of its body is a muscular mass that drives the huge tail. A blue whale can travel at 25 miles per hour, making it the swiftest of the great whales.

The blue whale holds the record as the fastest-growing animal. During an 11-month gestation a baby blue grows from a single cell to 25 feet long and 6,600 pounds at birth. It may put on as much as 200 pounds a day sucking its mother's milk. At 2 years old, the calf may already be 75 feet long and weigh 250,000 pounds, larger than any other whale species. The blue whale may live as long as 90 years.

Like the bowhead whale, the blue whale is a

SPERM WHALE (cont.)

OUTLINE OF THROAT AT
FULLEST EXTENSION

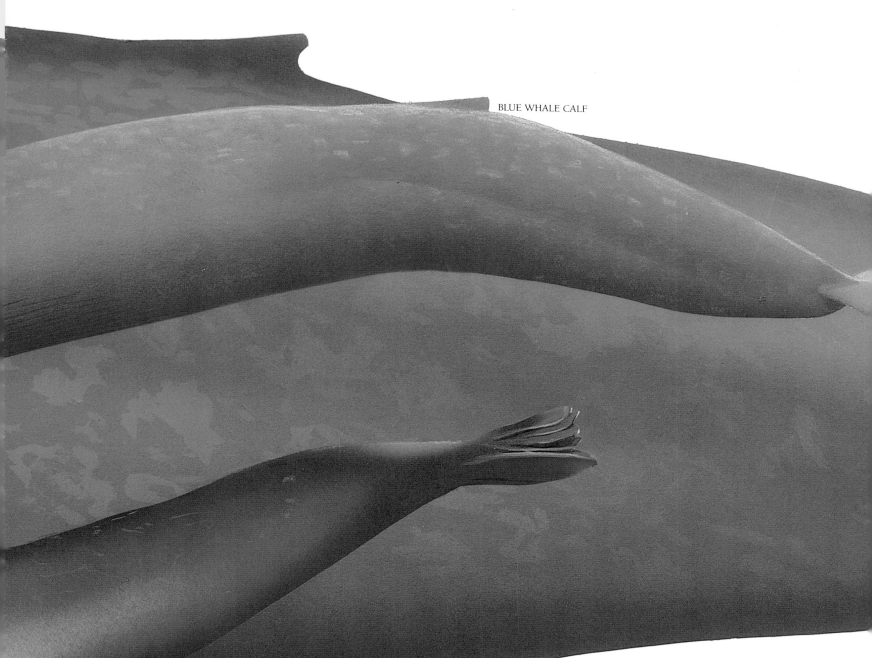

BLUE WHALE CALF

BLUE WHALE (cont.)

average bull measures 16½ feet with a weight of 5,000 pounds; females usually measure 11 feet and weigh 2,000 pounds. The bull's long nose droops many inches below its mouth and resembles an elephant's trunk. The nose inflates as the bull roars to settle territorial disputes or guard its harem of females, called cows. After an 11-month gestation, cows give birth to 4-foot-long, 80-pound pups.

The elephant seal is wrapped in a thick blanket of blubber that insulates it and streamlines its shape. Its rear flippers point straight back and propel it through the water while the front flippers steer. The elephant seal's preferred prey is the rat-fish, a species that lives only below 300 feet. The elephant seal's large eyes are well adapted for seeing in the deep, dimly lit water in which it feeds.

Northern elephant seals live in Pacific coastal waters and congregate on sandy beaches in the summer to shed. Unlike other animals that shed a few hairs at a time, the elephant seal sheds its entire skin in large patches. On land the elephant seal is a sluggish animal, moving about by contracting its belly muscles in a rippling fashion. Hunted nearly to extinction, elephant seals are now protected by law. Its enemies are humans and the great white shark.

OUTLINE OF THROAT AT
FULLEST EXTENSION

NORTHERN ELEPHANT SEAL

Northern Elephant Seal

Mirounga angustirostris
Carnivora • Mammalia • Chordata

The elephant seal is the largest of the pinnipeds, marine carnivores with all four limbs evolved into flippers. The northern elephant seal is somewhat bigger than the southern. The northern male, known as a bull, may grow as large as 22½ feet long and may weigh up to 9,000 pounds. The

Bowhead Whale

Balaena mysticetus
Cetacea • Mammalia • Chordata

Also known as the Greenland right whale, the bowhead is named for the great arch of its skull, which accounts for almost a third of its length. The largest bowheads may reach up to 67 feet in length and weigh 268,000 pounds. Like all whales, the bowhead must periodically surface to breathe air.

Although some whales have teeth, the bowhead has baleen, special horny filters that hang in sheets from its upper jaws. Bowheads eat plankton, the soup of tiny floating plants and animals (especially krill, a type of shrimp) that accumulate near the ocean's surface. Swimming slowly through plankton-rich seawater with its huge mouth wide open, the bowhead periodically closes its mouth and pushes the water through the baleen filters with its 8,000-pound tongue. The plankton remains trapped on the baleen's hairy inner fringes, ready to be licked off. The bowhead has 12-foot-long baleen, the longest of any whale.

The bowhead whale is comfortably blanketed from the bone-chilling waters of its home in the Arctic Ocean with blubber 2 feet thick. The bowhead and its relative, the right whale, are slow and tend not to sink after being harpooned; hence they were the "right" whales to chase. After being hunted nearly to extinction, the bowhead is now protected by law.

Zeuglodon

Zeuglodon cetoides   [extinct]
Cetacea • Mammalia • Chordata

Zeuglodon (ZOO-glow-don) reached sizes of up to 80 feet and 120,000 pounds, with 50 feet as an average length. Not an ancestor of modern whales but an evolutionary offshoot, *Zeuglodon* existed only during the early Eocene period, about 54 million years ago. *Zeuglodon* had a body resembling that of a modern whale, but its disproportionately small head remained very much like those of its ancestors, the early flesh-eating mammals.

Zeuglodon had a narrow skull with 44 variously shaped teeth designed to catch and crush hard-bodied mollusks and crustaceans. Its nostrils were midway between the tip of the snout and the top of the head. Like a whale's, *Zeuglodon*'s front

ZEUGLODON

limbs had evolved into flippers, but each flipper had an elbow joint that could still be pivoted, like a seal's.

Zeuglodon may have rested its long body in the sandy shallows of warm coastal waters, dipping its head below the surface to eat. Fossils, originally named *Basilosaurus* ("king of the reptiles"), were discovered in Louisiana in 1832.

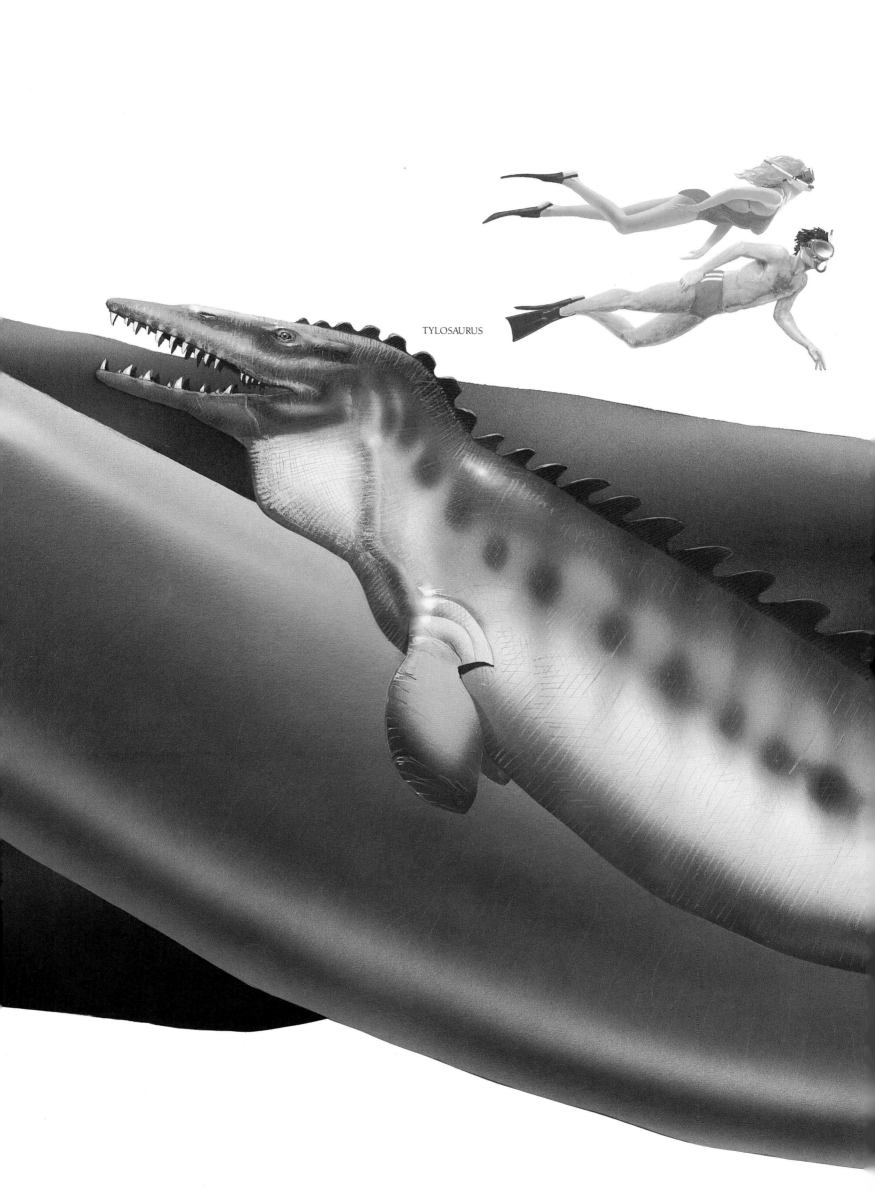

TYLOSAURUS

Tylosaurus

Tylosaurus dyspelor   [extinct]
Squamata • Reptilia • Chordata

Tylosaurus (tie-luh-SOR-uss) was a marine lizard of the Cretaceous period, 100 million years ago, that grew up to 45 feet long. A recently discovered close relative may have been 56 feet long. *Tylosaurus* was one of the largest mosasaurs, or sea lizards, related more closely to present-day lizards than to the pliosaurs they resembled or to any of the dinosaurs.

Tylosaurus's body and tail were flattened from side to side and it swam by making back-and-forth undulations like a sea snake. The thin, webbed flippers were small and were used only for steering. *Tylosaurus* had large, conical teeth for catching fish and crushing shelled sea creatures. The lower jaw had an extra joint midway down its length, enabling *Tylosaurus* to open its jaws extra wide. Its nostrils were situated on top of its head, like a whale's, enabling *Tylosaurus* to breathe while remaining almost completely submerged. Fossils have been found in northern Europe and Kansas.

BOWHEAD WHALE (cont.)

ZEUGLODON (cont.)

Steller's Sea Cow

Rhytina stelleri [extinct]
Sirenia • Mammalia • Chordata

Once found only in the frigid waters around islands in the Bering Strait between Alaska and the Soviet Union, Steller's sea cow was the largest of the Sirenia, plant-eating mammals probably related more closely to elephants than to the seals, walruses, and whales they resemble. From 28 to 35 feet long, Steller's sea cow, like its smaller cousins the manatee and dugong, had a front like a walrus's and a tail like a whale's. The head held two tiny eyes, almost hidden among the wrinkles and rolls of blubber. Its huge, split upper lip, studded with long, strong bristles, was used to nip off seaweed. It was always eating to support its huge bulk. Steller's sea cows lived in herds. They were often seen to float vertically with their heads held high out of the water.

In 1742, Georg Wilhelm Steller, a German doctor with the first Russian expedition to the area, became the only trained scientist ever to see a Steller's sea cow alive. There may have been as few as 1,500 individuals left at the time. By 1770 the peaceful sea cows had been slaughtered to extinction for their meat.

STELLER'S SEA COW

ZEUGLODON (cont.)

Sea Scorpion

Pterygotus buffalohensis [extinct]
Eurypterida • Chelicerata • Arthropoda

The sea scorpion, a meat-eating underwater relative of the modern horseshoe crab, grew up to 9 feet long. It lived in coastal lagoons 500 to 360 million years ago, from the Ordovician through the Devonian period. It probably preyed on the very first vertebrates, seeking them with its many-faceted eyes and snatching them with huge pincers called chelicerae, which were not limbs but extended mouth parts positioned in front of the first pair of limbs. Scientists believe that the sea scorpion crawled rightside up but swam upside down. Like the horseshoe crab, its paddle-shaped rear limbs moved like oars and the plates on its belly fanned the water. Its flattened tail could have been flapped for rapid acceleration toward prey or away from predators. Fossils have been found in North America, Australia, and Europe.

Dinichthys

Dinichthys terrelli [extinct]
Arthrodira • Placodermi • Chordata

Dinichthys (die-NIK-thiss) was one of the largest of the placoderms, prehistoric fish that had bony armor protecting the forward parts of the head and body. The largest *Dinichthys* grew up to 30 feet long and was one of the biggest animals of the Devonian period, some 350 million years ago.

Dinichthys was a ferocious predator that ate primitive sharks and armored fish. Its powerful jaws could crack their armor. *Dinichthys* had no true teeth. Instead, fanglike projections of sharp bone jutted out from its jaws to serve the same purpose. Bone enveloped its head and the forward portions of its back, and a flattened chest plate protected it underneath. Even its large eyes were protected by a ring of bone. The rest of its body was without armor. *Dinichthys* swam with side-to-side sweeping movements of its long tail and used its fins for steering. Fossils have been found in Europe and North America.

Giant Spider Crab

Macrocheira kaempferi
Decapoda • Crustacea • Arthropoda

Sometimes called the stilt crab, the giant spider crab is the largest living arthropod, cold-blooded animals with hard coverings of chitin over their segmented bodies and many-jointed legs. The crab's body is only 12 to 14 inches long, but the span from pincer to pincer can measure up to 12 feet, and unconfirmed measurements of 19 feet have been reported. The giant spider crab can weigh up to 41 pounds.

Found in the deep seas surrounding Japan, the giant spider crab has small, 5-inch pincers at the ends of its enormously long arms. They are used in fighting, digging burrows, and catching fish. The crab's long legs help it to walk through the soft ooze of the deep-sea bottom.

SEA SCORPION

DINICHTHYS

Archelon

Archelon ischyros   [extinct]
Chelonia • Reptilia • Chordata

Archelon (AR-kuh-lon), a giant marine turtle of the Cretaceous period 70 million years ago, was the largest turtle ever, measuring up to 14 feet long and weighing up to 4,000 pounds. The largest living sea turtle, the leatherback, measures up to 8 feet 4 inches long and weighs up to 1,908 pounds.

The ancestors of *Archelon* were land turtles, which evolved flippers as they became seagoing reptiles. Like that of the leatherback, *Archelon*'s back consisted of a framework, not a solid mass, of widened ribs and backbone, and its "shell" was a tough layer of skin, in place of the horny shell of enlarged scales present on most other turtles. Like all turtles, *Archelon* had no teeth, but its jaws were powerful and sharp, with hooked tips. It ate shellfish, fish, and some plants. *Archelon* had to surface periodically to breathe and probably came ashore only to lay eggs, like a modern sea turtle.

ARCHELON

GIANT SPIDER CRAB

GIANT SQUID

Arctic Lion's Mane Jellyfish

Cyanea capillata arctica
Semaeostomae • Scyphozoa • Coelenterata

Found in all northern waters and named for its dusky yellow fringe of tentacles, the Arctic lion's mane jellyfish is by far the largest jellyfish in the world. The bell of this giant can be 7½ feet wide, and the streaming tentacles can extend for 120 feet. There are reports of specimens with tentacles 275 feet long, but these are consid-

Giant Squid

Architeuthis dux
Decapoda • Cephalopoda • Mollusca

The giant squid may reach a length of 55 feet, including its 35-foot tentacles, and may weigh up to 4,480 pounds. Giant specimens are rare; 6½ footers are the common variety. Giant squids are found in all the oceans, but the largest live at the extreme depths of the North Atlantic, where light cannot penetrate and humans rarely venture.

The giant squid has eight thick arms and two slender tentacles. The arms are double-lined with sucking disks for seizing and holding prey. The tentacles, with sucking disks clustered at the enlarged ends, are used to shoot out and grab prey, pulling it back within range of the arms. The giant squid has a horny, parrotlike, beaked mouth in the center of its arms and a rasping tongue called a radula. Its eyes, among the most advanced of invertebrates, may measure up to 9 inches across.

The giant squid's rocket-shaped body has fins on the back end and is stiffened by an internal layer of horny material. The animal swims slowly, with rippling movements of its fins, but it may jet away with incredible acceleration by forcibly ejecting water out a mobile funnel below the head. The funnel is flexible so that the squid can accelerate in any direction and make sharp turns as well. The giant squid may also eject a foul, inky fluid that acts as a smoke screen to confuse its enemy, the sperm whale, which often bears circular scars left by the squid's sawtooth-edged suckers.

ered unreliable. Typically the Arctic lion's mane jellyfish has a bell 3 feet wide, and its 1,200 tentacles may reach 75 feet in length. It is futile to remove a giant jellyfish from the water to weigh or measure it. Only two layers of cells make up the body, and it disintegrates without the support of water all around.

This jellyfish swims by drawing its body together and expelling the water within the bell. Both food and waste materials pass through the mouth, the only opening in the body, located beneath the central umbrella. The Arctic lion's mane jellyfish eats any small marine organism that swims too close to the poisonous stinging cells on its long tentacles, which may be fatal to human swimmers as well. To capture prey, this giant jellyfish sinks slowly with its tentacles spread out in a wide net covering over 500 square yards. On contact, a stinging tentacle contracts to $\frac{1}{10}$ its size in less than a second, bringing the prey within reach of curtainlike oral arms. These draw the victim up to the mouth to be digested.

Jellyfish are among the most ancient of animals, leaving fossil impressions that date from some 750 million years ago.

GLOSSARY

amphibians Cold-blooded backboned animals that breathe with gills underwater until maturity and breathe air as adults; includes frogs and salamanders.

arthropods Cold-blooded backboneless animals with a shell and jointed legs, such as insects, shrimp, and crabs.

baleen "Teeth" that hang from a whale's jaws in large sheets to form a sieve for filtering food from seawater.

canine teeth The large pointed teeth between the front teeth (incisors) and back teeth (molars) in mammals.

carnivores Meat-eating mammals.

carrion Dead and decaying flesh.

cartilage Whitish, tough yet flexible tissue that supports and shapes many parts of the body, but is not as rigid as bone.

chitin A hornlike substance that forms the shells of insects, crabs, and other arthropods.

Chordata Animals that breathe with gills or lungs and also have a spinal cord, perhaps with a backbone to protect it.

Coelenterata Simple backboneless animals consisting of little more than skin, tentacles, mouth, and stomach; includes jellyfish.

cold-blooded An animal whose body temperature rises or falls along with the temperature of its surroundings.

crustaceans Arthropods with many jointed legs and two pairs of antennae, such as crabs.

depth perception The ability to judge the distance of objects from oneself.

dinosaurs Extinct land reptiles, usually large, with legs placed directly under their bodies instead of splayed out to the sides.

dorsal fin A fin on the back of an animal, usually an aquatic one.

echolocation See sonar.

embryo An unborn animal during the earliest stages of its development.

evolution The history of the gradual change and development of different species.

extendable jaws A mouth with special joints that let it open very wide to take in food.

extinct No longer existing; specifically, when all of the individuals of a particular species are presumed to be dead.

fossil The remains of a living thing that have turned to stone.

gestation The gradual development of the young within the body of the mother before birth.

gills The blood-filled organs that most fish and young amphibians use to obtain oxygen from water for breathing.

incubate To keep an egg warm so it will hatch.

insulation A covering like feathers, hair, or blubber that keeps an animal warm.

invertebrates Animals without a backbone.

mammals Warm-blooded backboned animals that feed their young with milk from the mother's body, such as humans, bears, and whales.

marsupials Mammals whose females have an external pouch for carrying the underdeveloped young; includes kangaroos.

mollusks Cold-blooded backboneless animals with soft bodies that are usually enclosed in a hard shell, such as clams, snails, and (shell-less) squids.

nocturnal Active at night.

nymph Immature insect young, usually without wings.

plankton Small- to microscopic-size plants and animals that float in water.

predator An animal that kills other animals for food.

prehensile An organ, such as a hand, that can grasp or wrap around an object.

prehistoric The time before written languages existed.

primates Mammals with nails, not claws; forward-looking eyes; prehensile hands, and sometimes prehensile feet and tails, too.

reptiles Cold-blooded air-breathing backboned animals that are usually covered with scales, such as snakes and turtles.

resonating chamber A space inside an animal that amplifies sounds, usually for mating calls.

scavenger An animal that feeds on animals it finds already dead.

serrated Having tiny saw-like teeth on an edge for improved cutting.

sexual maturity The age when male and female animals develop the ability to mate and produce young.

sonar A way of detecting objects by sending out a series of sounds and then listening for the echos reflecting off the object.

species A group of animals or plants with similar characteristics and the ability to breed with one another and reproduce themselves; the basic unit of scientific classification.

vertebrae The bones of the backbone, from the neck bones to the tail bones.

vertebrates Animals with a backbone made of bone or cartilage.

vestigial digit A finger or toe that is so small and poorly developed that it is of practically no use.

warm-blooded Animals with the ability to create and maintain body heat regardless of the temperature of the surroundings.

GIANT SQUID (cont.)

INDEX TO THE ANIMALS

Page numbers in *italic type* refer to material in illustrations.

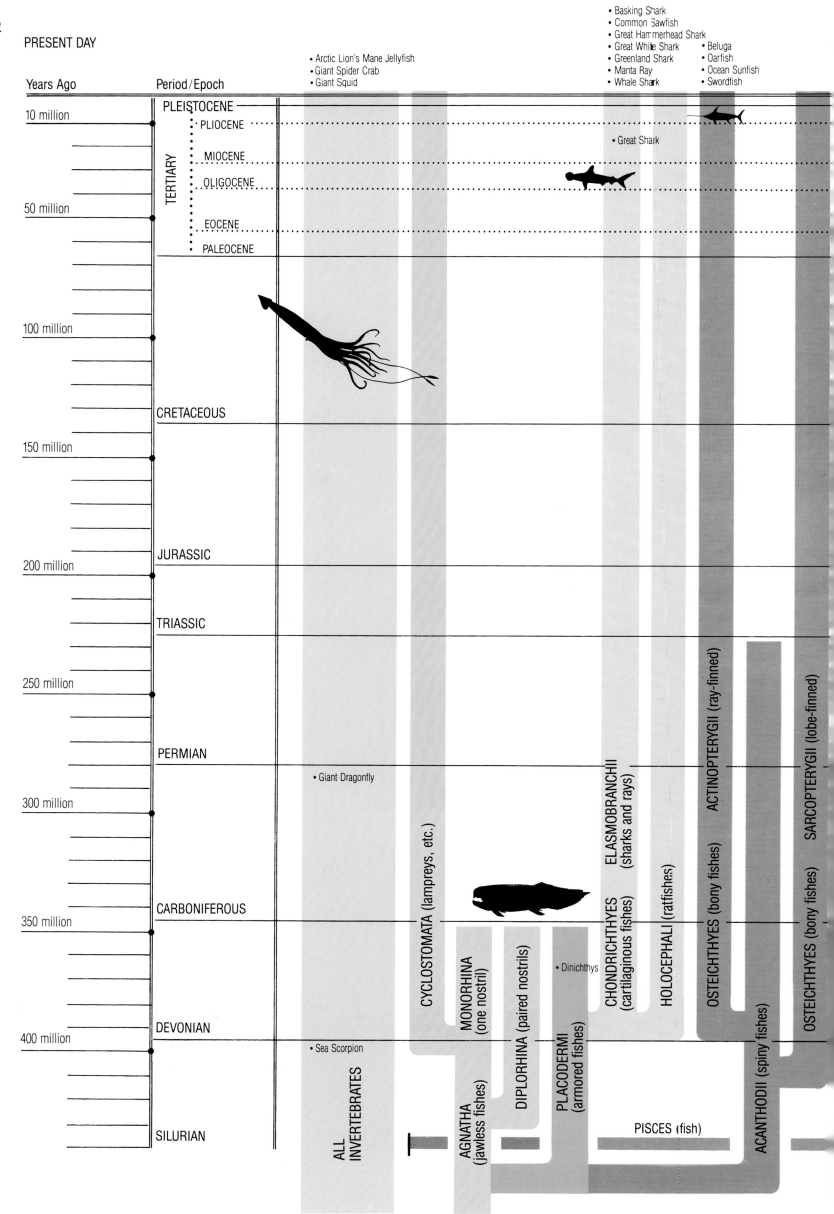

PRESENT DAY

Years Ago   Period/Epoch

- Basking Shark
- Common Sawfish
- Great Hammerhead Shark
- Great White Shark   • Beluga
- Greenland Shark   • Oarfish
- Manta Ray   • Ocean Sunfish
- Whale Shark   • Swordfish

- Arctic Lion's Mane Jellyfish
- Giant Spider Crab
- Giant Squid

10 million   PLEISTOCENE
                    PLIOCENE
50 million   TERTIARY   MIOCENE
                            OLIGOCENE   • Great Shark
                            EOCENE
                            PALEOCENE
100 million   CRETACEOUS
150 million
200 million   JURASSIC
                TRIASSIC
250 million
                PERMIAN
                                • Giant Dragonfly
300 million
                CARBONIFEROUS   • Dinichthys
350 million
                DEVONIAN
400 million   • Sea Scorpion
                SILURIAN

ALL INVERTEBRATES

CYCLOSTOMATA (lampreys, etc.)

AGNATHA (jawless fishes)

MONORHINA (one nostril)

DIPLORHINA (paired nostrils)

PLACODERMI (armored fishes)

CHONDRICHTHYES (cartilaginous fishes)

ELASMOBRANCHII (sharks and rays)

HOLOCEPHALI (ratfishes)

OSTEICHTHYES (bony fishes)

ACTINOPTERYGII (ray-finned)

ACANTHODII (spiny fishes)

OSTEICHTHYES (bony fishes)

SARCOPTERYGII (lobe-finned)

OSTEICHTHYES (bony fishes)

PISCES (fish)

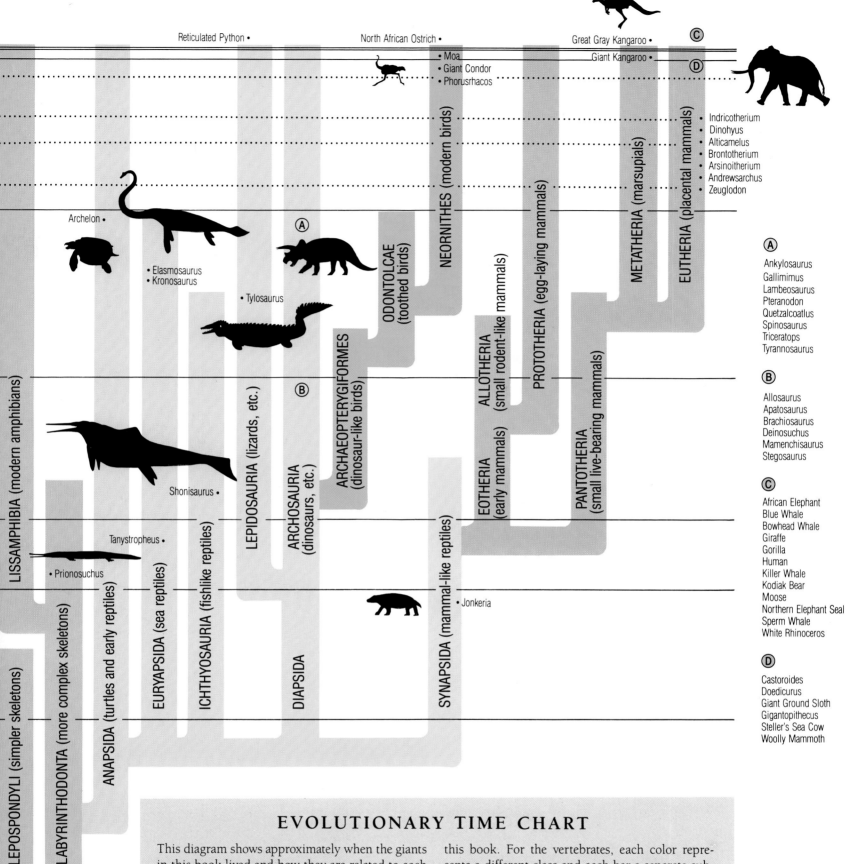

Reticulated Python •

North African Ostrich •

Great Gray Kangaroo •

Ⓒ

Giant Kangaroo •

Ⓓ

• Moa
• Giant Condor
• Phorusrhacos

• Indricotherium
• Dinohyus
• Alticamelus
• Brontotherium
• Arsinoitherium
• Andrewsarchus
• Zeuglodon

Archelon •

• Elasmosaurus
• Kronosaurus

Ⓐ

• Tylosaurus

Shonisaurus •

Ⓑ

Tanystropheus •

• Prionosuchus

• Jonkeria

LEPOSPONDYLI (simpler skeletons)

LABYRINTHODONTA (more complex skeletons)

LISSAMPHIBIA (modern amphibians)

ANAPSIDA (turtles and early reptiles)

EURYAPSIDA (sea reptiles)

ICHTHYOSAURIA (fishlike reptiles)

LEPIDOSAURIA (lizards, etc.)

DIAPSIDA

ARCHOSAURIA (dinosaurs, etc.)

ARCHAEOPTERYGIFORMES (dinosaur-like birds)

ODONTOLCAE (toothed birds)

NEORNITHES (modern birds)

SYNAPSIDA (mammal-like reptiles)

EOTHERIA (early mammals)

ALLOTHERIA (small rodent-like mammals)

PANTOTHERIA (small live-bearing mammals)

PROTOTHERIA (egg-laying mammals)

METATHERIA (marsupials)

EUTHERIA (placental mammals)

Ⓐ

Ankylosaurus
Gallimimus
Lambeosaurus
Pteranodon
Quetzalcoatlus
Spinosaurus
Triceratops
Tyrannosaurus

Ⓑ

Allosaurus
Apatosaurus
Brachiosaurus
Deinosuchus
Mamenchisaurus
Stegosaurus

Ⓒ

African Elephant
Blue Whale
Bowhead Whale
Giraffe
Gorilla
Human
Killer Whale
Kodiak Bear
Moose
Northern Elephant Seal
Sperm Whale
White Rhinoceros

Ⓓ

Castoroides
Doedicurus
Giant Ground Sloth
Gigantopithecus
Steller's Sea Cow
Woolly Mammoth

EVOLUTIONARY TIME CHART

This diagram shows approximately when the giants in this book lived and how they are related to each other. The animals that are alive today are all listed at the top of the chart, no matter how long ago they evolved. The extinct animals are located only roughly in their proper time because of lack of space; more exact dates are given in the text.

The invertebrates have been grouped together in one color bar because there are so few of them in this book. For the vertebrates, each color represents a different class and each bar a separate subclass or smaller group.

The color bars extend up to the present as long as at least one member of a branch is still alive. This means, for example, that the archosaur line still exists (in the form of a few species of crocodilians) even though the dinosaurs died out millions of years ago.

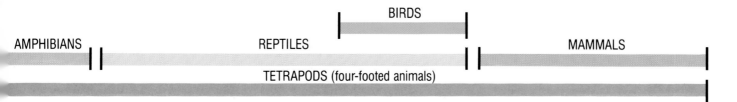

BIRDS

AMPHIBIANS

REPTILES

MAMMALS

TETRAPODS (four-footed animals)

David Peters is a St. Louis–based freelance commercial artist who is self-taught. He graduated from the School of Journalism at the University of Missouri in Columbia. Like many children, he had an early interest in dinosaurs, whales, and sharks, and at the age of 31 expressed his interest in this, his first book.